LIVING *by*

Los Dichos

LIVING *by* Los Dichos

Advice from a Mother to a Daughter

CRISTINA PÉREZ

ATRIA BOOKS

New York   London   Toronto   Sydney

ATRIA BOOKS

1230 Avenue of the Americas
New York, NY 10020

Copyright © 2006 by Cristina Pérez Gonzalez

Library of Congress Cataloging-in-Publication Data

Pérez, Cristina.
    Living by los dichos: advice from a mother to a daughter / Cristina Pérez.
    1st Atria Books trade pbk. ed.
       p. cm.
    Includes bibliographical references.
    1. Conduct of life. 2. Latin Americans—Quotations. 3. Hispanic
Americans—Conduct of life.
    I. Title
    BJ1521.P34   2006

                                                        2006042934

ISBN-13: 978-0-7432-8778-4
ISBN-10:   0-7432-8778-9

First Atria Books trade paperback edition September 2006

10 9 8 7 6 5 4 3 2 1

ATRIA BOOKS is a trademark of Simon & Schuster, Inc.

Manufactured in the United States of America

For information about special discounts for bulk purchases,
please contact Simon & Schuster Special Sales at
1-800-456-6798 or business@simonandschuster.com.

*I dedicate this book to my daughter, Sofia Daniella,
so that she may never forget where she came from and
always follow the path her heart desires.*

*And to Ray, my number one fan. I know you're
wheeling and dealing for me in Heaven.*

Contents

INTRODUCTION

When Hollywood Calls on Tradition

"El que es buen juez, por su casa empieza"
(Being a good judge starts at home)

I'm sure that the original meaning of this traditional saying has nothing to do with being on a TV court show, but it really is the perfect description of my experiences in that industry. Words like "tradition," "family," and "values" aren't typically associated with mainstream Hollywood. I think it's exactly *because* I represent and advocate these three ideals that Hollywood initially called on me.

I had never really thought about a television career and I have to admit that I wasn't particularly attracted to it. Nowhere in my right mind did I ever think I would be on television—even though my mother always said that she knew I would be. Of course she did. What mother wouldn't expect her own child to succeed? However, my first television job, a Spanish court program called *La Corte de Familia (The Family Court),* came into my life completely out of the blue.

As an immigration lawyer, I deal with various notable clients in the entertainment and athletic industries and their representatives. I had a client, a producer, who worked with one of the producers of *La Corte de Familia,* and I soon came to know both of them. At the time we met, they had a local show on the air in Los Angeles and were looking for a new "judge" to host it. My client and his producer friend quickly recommended me for the position and I was called in to try out—oh, sorry, to perform a screen test, as they say in the "industry." I did so, reluctantly and also a little fearfully—me, on TV? To convince myself, I decided it would be a great opportunity to tell my kids and grandkids about my big Hollywood screen test. I found myself auditioning alongside the most notable Latino lawyers in Los Angeles—no pressure, right? But I was the one those producers called the next day—I got the job!

They said they liked me because I represented the traditional values of the Latino community, yet interpreted them in a modern way that would connect with today's Latino and American viewers. Young, hip, and modern, yet traditional and conservative, I represented all generations equally. I was the walking, talking, teaching combination of all worlds.

Filming a court TV show was truly an adventure and a challenge. The show was in Spanish and I always jokingly say that I'm like half-and-half—fifty-fifty English and Spanish. The fact that I was caught between both worlds and both languages played out on the show—sometimes humorously. For instance, the one word I consistently had trouble with was *veredicto* (verdict). Imagine, the one word a judge says the most, and I couldn't seem to spit it out when the cameras were rolling. Sure, turn the cameras off and I could reel off *veredicto* after *veredicto* until the cows came home. I guess I was suffering from an unusual and untimely case of stage fright.

We shot the show locally in Los Angeles for a year before the network purchased it, essentially promoting me from local to international network television. Pretty good for a newbie, huh? Even with all this newfound recognition, I was pleased and I'm sure my family was too to note that I didn't change as a person. Sure, my "on camera" personality was sometimes a more exaggerated version of myself. Television calls for something bigger, so all I had to do was raise the volume on my already amplified "Latina charisma." After all, if I changed anything else about myself other than that and possibly the color of my nail polish, my mother would have come clear across my TV courtroom to knock our family values right back into me!

In my over five years filming *La Corte de Familia* I discovered an empowering aspect of the entertainment industry that I enjoy. I've found that my Spanish-speaking fans are like my extended family. When my fans meet me, they're respectful and say hello as if they have known me for years. The power of the media—television and print—is amazing. Is there a better way to reach out to your community than appearing in a little electronic box in their living room every day, speaking to them in their language? Working in the media gives me the ability to defend what is important to my community. I feel a responsibility to my culture. Simply by showing my face on television, I am instantly a messenger for the people that I represent.

When I began to write this book, I was filming a new court television pilot for a major American television network. As I end it, I am now set to star in a new show called *Cristina's Court* for FOX Television. The story of how this came to fruition is remarkably similar to the story of how *La Corte de Familia* came into my life. My agent introduced me to a television director looking for a new female Latina "judge." While having lunch with that director and getting to know him, I suddenly had a remarkable realization. This man, this stranger across the table, had exactly the same values as my father. He had the warmth, the sincerity, and the faith in me that my father has always had. Of course we hit it off instantly. The director introduced me to FOX and just like that Spanish network all those years ago, this new network also liked what I stand for. They immediately saw that I am a traditional yet mainstream Latina.

In other words, the identity instilled in me by my parents every day is still shining through as bright as ever. I walked into FOX as myself, just the way my parents raised me. I stayed true to myself—living by *los dichos* and all the other cultural traditions and values I learned from my mother and father. And that's exactly what those executives were looking for.

SECTION I

Defining Los Dichos

CHAPTER ONE

De mi vida para tu vida

"No hay boca donde no esté,
ni lengua ni país que desconozca,
ni sabiduría que lo sustituya."

(There is no mouth where it is not present,
Neither language nor country it does not know,
No wisdom can replace it.)

—Luís A. Acuna

Learning Los Dichos

I have to admit that I'm not an expert, I'm not a doctor, and I'm not a therapist. I'm just a woman, a mother, a wife, and a professional who lives and learns from her experiences, her mistakes, her family, and her culture. This is my version of a guidebook based on my life—from relationships and family to work and cultural identity issues and everything in between! I'm going to cover all the lessons that I learned from my mother and am now passing along to my daughter. I hope that mothers and daughters everywhere can find something in this book to enrich their lives and then pass along to their children.

As you will discover, this book, like my life, is premised on the solid fundamental teachings and lessons I have learned through *dichos* and wisdom from my family. I choose to use dichos because they are a symbolic vehicle for relatively simple concepts that guide me through certain situations in life. Each chapter includes symbolic dichos relevant to the chapter's content, with my interpretation of them, how I have applied them, and how you the reader can use the dichos to enhance your own life. While I provide an English translation of each dicho, it may not be literal. What I am providing is the moral of each dicho.

"Lo que bien se aprende, nunca se pierde"
(What is well learned is never lost)

In order for a culture to have any kind of longevity, its participants must actively study each stitch of thread that has created the culture and holds it together. Both young and old should learn and live by their culture's wisdom so that it can continue to flourish for future generations. Every culture possesses its own way of passing this wisdom on from generation to generation.

In the Latino culture, dichos act as that intergenerational gateway. Dichos are invaluable proverbs and sayings that succinctly deliver a serious message, value, or belief. They are used to help make a point, teach a life lesson, and validate life's trials and tribulations. Dichos serve as profound lessons to be learned from the life experiences of our forefathers, each incorporating the astuteness of past generations and serving as teaching tools for us to live by today and tomorrow. In learning and living by *los dichos* we continually breathe life into the inspiring, humorous, and philosophical proverbs that have woven themselves throughout Latino culture for centuries while being blind to educational, economic, and class systems. Dichos are history translated into words.

Thousands of dichos exist—some humorous, some serious, and some specific to certain countries. Each has a particular meaning that is generally universal and crosses over all cultures.

Dichos provide messages of hope, direction, and guidance just when we need them. When for some reason or another a basic truth escapes us, dichos put us back on track. When we face challenges, dichos offer clarity and direction.

Because of these reasons and many more, dichos are the rules that I live by everyday.

"De tal palo, tal astilla"
(The apple does not fall far from the tree)

This dicho is similar to the English sayings "The apple does not fall far from the tree" and "Like father like son." My parents migrated to the United States from Colombia in the 1960s. They came to this country with essentially nothing except each other and the dream of a better life for themselves and their children. My father is from a large family of modest means, with thirteen brothers and sisters. In fact, my grandmother, my father's mother, was pregnant twenty-two times. My mother is also from a large family of eleven brothers and sisters. My family is a walking and talking billboard for the big Latino family.

Shortly after they were married, my parents decided to move to the United States "temporarily," as is frequently the intention of many immigrants. Their plan was to work and save enough money to one day send my father to medical school and return to Colombia. Forty-plus years later our family is still here.

Darío's Story

My father's dream was to become a doctor like his uncle in Colombia, whom he worked for as a young man. The United States, as my father puts it, was the land of "possibility and potential." So he and my mother arrived in Bronx, New York, in 1963, in a country where he and my mother did not know a soul. The idea was to stay for six months and find work. If my father could not find work, then they planned to return home.

An educated man, my father looked for a job wherever he could. His English was not the best, but good enough. However, it seemed that no one had any available openings that he could fill. He recalls being turned away the moment the potential employer looked at him or heard him speak. He resorted to employment agencies that were also of no help.

Finally, he found a job at a hospital, in housekeeping, and worked as a janitor. The hospital was one and a half hours away from the Bronx. He earned fifty dollars a week and would spend at least one third of his pay traveling to and from the job, so he was forced to live at housing provided by the hospital. He visited my mother only on the weekends. At the time, she was pregnant with my sister.

After a short while, my father decided he needed a better job and for thirty days, he walked the streets searching. He finally found a new job with a watch company in Manhattan and was able to reunite with my mother. He also moved her to a safer neighborhood in Queens. My father worked there for over five years doing piecework on an assembly line. At this time, the watch company contracted with the United States government to make, among other things, timers for bazookas used in the Vietnam War.

My father felt like he experienced plenty of discrimination at this job from other employees who had been working there for a long time. The most senior pieceworkers were comfortable in their environment and the guy who produced the most pieces was admired as the "stud" of the workplace. When my father came along, he believed that the senior workers were threatened by this new one-man workforce. You see, my father the future surgeon, was very good with his hands and worked fast. Instead of respecting him for his good work they made fun of him. They would chastise him, saying things like, "Of course he has to work fast! He can't speak English very well so that's all he has to do." My father didn't take it personally because he knew that job was a stepping stone, but for the other workers it may have been their final destination. Nevertheless, the workers made it so uncomfortable for my father that the supervisor finally told him, "Don't worry about these jokers. If you can make more pieces than anyone else, do it because we pay by the piece. Knock yourself out." He received $1.79 per one thousand pieces. The average worker made 1,000 to 1,200 pieces per hour. My father knew he had to push himself to provide for his growing family (my brother had arrived by then), and to realize his dream of becoming a surgeon. He pushed himself to produce over 2,300 pieces per hour.

While working full time, he decided to enroll full time at Manhattan Medical School to become a laboratory technician. After graduating, my father, finally armed with improved credentials, was able to obtain better paying jobs with different hospitals in New York City and eventually became a laboratory supervisor at a blood bank.

My father's principal goal during this time was to move his family to a better neighborhood. After continually being told he could not afford it with only fifty dollars in his checking account, he bought our first home in Bethpage, New York. He borrowed all he could and for the next five years he worked two full-time jobs and one part-time job until he paid off his loans. He even managed to save enough money for medical school.

At that moment my father felt that he had worked enough—it was time to obtain his medical degree and become a doctor. He reminded himself of his goal: "I came to the United States to find work, make money, and pursue my goal of becoming a doctor." Obviously, he could have just continued working for the rest of his life at jobs that paid the bills and supported his family but did little else. He asked himself, "Why did I come to America?" He feared that he had almost given up his dream for the complacency of the daily grind. Enough of that! It was time to go for it.

With a family of five to support, attending medical school in the United States was financially out of the question. In the early 1970s, he applied to foreign medical schools in Guadalajara, Mexico, and in Salamanca, Spain. It was more cost effective to maintain a family abroad while attending medical school on a full-time basis. Spain was not an option, as the travel cost would break him financially. So he decided to attend the Universidad Autónoma de Medicina in Guadalajara, Mexico, a university associated with the American Medical Association. We drove cross-country from New York to Mexico so my father could attend medical school.

In a short period my father had gone from a decent paycheck in an unsatisfying job to no paycheck at all in medical school, his dream. Now imagine this—he was a full-time student, had some money from student loans, but had no job to provide for his family of three children, all under the age of twelve, and a wife. How did he and my mother make it? Simple: during his vacations and holiday breaks from school, whether it was one or two weeks or summertime, my father would drive or fly, sometimes with the entire family, to the United States to work and save money to bring back to Mexico.

My father finally graduated from medical school on time in the late 1970s. But let me tell you, he did not just "gradu-

ate." Out of over nine hundred students, he was valedictorian
of his class. I remember that ceremony. I remember my
brother getting so mad about dressing up and wearing a
bowtie. I recall sitting in a room filled with over two thousand
people, in the front row with my family. I felt special. I
watched my stoic mother following my father with her eyes as
he so proudly and humbly took center stage. I have to be honest, I don't remember what he said. I can only imagine. But as
I look back on it today, I am convinced that this experience
was a defining moment in my life.

So you might think now that my father had really made
it—he was a doctor, and an educated man. He could find
work anywhere, right? Wrong! Upon returning to the United
States as a foreign medical graduate, my father faced other
forms of discrimination. You see, there appears to be an unwritten, backroom, behind closed doors policy to discrimi-
nate against foreign medical doctors, regardless of nationality.
As my father explains, and I witnessed firsthand, the feeling
from the American medical community is that the training
and education received by foreign doctors is inferior to that
received by doctors educated and trained in the United
States.

To compensate for this perceived inferiority, after graduating from medical school my father was required to complete
two years of *servicio social* (social service). He was accepted at a
respected hospital in Tijuana, Mexico. So we moved again,
this time into low-income housing ("the projects") in San
Ysidro, California, a developing community at the time. San
Ysidro is located in the most southern part of San Diego on

the Mexican border, the busiest international border crossing in the world. San Ysidro was then and remains now very ethnically diverse. During our two years there, we met people from all walks of life. It was particularly exciting because we were exposed to a culture that was half American and half Mexican.

While working in the hospital, my father again struggled as a medical resident, working endless hours (usually on call for up to fifty-eight hours at a time), studying for exams, and providing for his family. In addition, my father had to work across the border in Tijuana. Because of this hectic schedule and the commute, he only saw us every four days. It was lonely for him, but he was comforted knowing that we were all together as a family. The experience was difficult but fruitful because it exposed him to every facet of medicine, and made him truly realize he was destined to become a surgeon.

After his two years of service in Mexico, my father was accepted to complete his surgical residency at a prestigious hospital on the east coast. We moved once again. From the outset, the chief of surgery gave my father a hard time. He had to constantly prove himself. Like many others at the time, this man probably thought that foreign medical graduates were not good enough to succeed in America. I remember my father coming home after feeling that his self-esteem was constantly being chipped away. I could see the frustration in his eyes and the disappointment in his face, and I heard it in his voice, that after all the obstacles he overcame he still wasn't being seen for his potential. He was still viewed as a foreigner, an immigrant first and a doctor second. I can't help but think that if I'm still having such a strong reaction to this, what must the impact have been on my father? What must he have felt in his gut and in his heart?

Time has since proven that foreign medical graduates have excelled in all areas of medicine, often overshadowing the accomplishments of their American-schooled counterparts. My father excelled here and eventually became the chief resident. In fact, my father was elected the best teaching resident by the medical students.

It took my father almost twenty years to accomplish his dream of becoming a surgeon, attaining the highest honor as a Diplomate of the American Board of Surgery. With great satisfaction, in the mid-1980s we moved to a Los Angeles suburb. My father established his medical practice in Glendale, California, where he still practices today. Consistently improving his medical skills and knowledge while achieving significant accomplishments along the way, he has won esteem and respect from the medical community, his peers, patients, friends, and family.

With my father's help, nine of his brothers and sisters eventually immigrated to the United States. As one of my uncles said to me, "Your father's titanic effort in coming to the United States in pursuit of a dream has been and will be the legacy and the definition of this family."

Aracelly's Story

My mother's experience, while similar to my father's, differed in many aspects. The move to the United States was emotionally challenging for her. With my father working, she was alone most of the time. She was also frustrated that she was not able to speak English well enough to communicate, frustrated because she was unfamiliar with the United States, its ways, culture, and customs, and made miserable by the severe cold and the severely warm humid New York weather. And she was scared of the future.

In New York, the neighborhood my parents initially lived in was not safe. My mother was pregnant and lived on the fifth floor of an apartment building with no elevator. Initially, she only saw my father on weekends. All she ever heard were sirens and at times she felt she was going crazy. It even crossed her mind to return to Colombia and wait for my father there. But she had promised to be with him during the good and the bad. How could she leave her husband alone? Her love and commitment to him carried her through many of these difficult times. Her mother's example and her religious and conservative upbringing allowed her to sacrifice for my father and her children. For her, family always comes first. She sounds too good to be true, right? You should meet the woman.

Eventually, my mother enrolled in English classes so the time would pass more quickly while she cared for her children. And yes, of course, she could work but who would take care of the children? Who would have the house clean and ready when her husband came home? Who would make him dinner after a long day of work? These were vitally important issues to her then and still are today. But it was hard for her to make friends because everyone always seemed busy. She was surrounded by Americans for whom English was a first language and who wouldn't give her the time of day. With no family members to talk to (her relatives were in Colombia and phone calls were an unattainable luxury), she felt like she was suffocating at times. But Guadalajara felt like home.

She could relate to the people, the culture, the traditions, and the language. In Guadalajara, my mother was able to work part time translating documents for medical students. But she believed her primary responsibilities were to take care of her husband, her three children, and her home. Our place in Guadalajara was always bustling with my father's friends; everyone was welcomed with open arms. After all, my father was the top student in his class and a great study partner. Despite the fact that my parents struggled, there was usually a home-cooked meal waiting for anyone who came to study or just to visit. My mother would say, *"Donde hay comida para uno, hay para dos, tres, cuatro . . ."* This meant where there is food for one there is food for two, three, or four.

Pretty quickly the Pérez Casa became *the* place for medical students to hang out. I've since asked my mother if this was a burden on her. She said, "No, on the contrary." She loved the company and loved to be able to support my father in any way she could, for these were precious times for him. She said it was our personality as a family that attracted so many to our home.

My mother further explains that although for over eleven years my father was essentially absent from our family, and she could have gotten upset, complained, and rebelled, but she did not. In her own words, she could not just think of herself. Her goal was to make it as easy as possible for my father to accomplish his lifelong dream. At the time, this was her sole purpose. My father worked so hard to become a physician in order to give us a better life. Unfortunately, this meant that he was often missing from our lives while we were growing up. Yet my mother managed to raise three children while carrying on the strong presence of my father in our home. She never let us forget our identity as a family. As she explains to me, she relied on the strength and wisdom she gained from her mother.

She acknowledges today that all of this was a risk because as a couple, they were becoming disconnected from each other. So she made sure she talked to my father and stayed connected by taking care of him and his family. It was her faith and trust in my father and the notion of family that empowered her, and most important, the love they have for each other that made her stick through it all. My mother did the best she could with what she had to work with. She always knew in her heart, guided by an unseen but deeply religious faith, while at the same time watching how hard my father worked, that everything would work out. She constantly had the intense faith that their dreams would come true.

I once asked my mother what living the American Dream meant to her. She said it meant my father becoming a surgeon and her children having good lives and pursuing their dreams. My mother raised us the only way she knew how—the way her mother and father raised her—with strong values and traditions. For example, she always wanted her children to speak Spanish as their first language. She clearly let me know that she is not and never was embarrassed or ashamed to be Latina. Even with her heavy accent, she made herself understood and still does today. Maintaining culture within her family was critical to my mother.

THE PÉREZ LEGACY

Through hard work and dedication, my parents made a better life for my family. They allowed us to develop a new identity in a new country. More important, they have given me access to better educational opportunities and a better way of life. My life was (and still is) so rich in many ways. In search of this better life my parents exposed my sister, brother, and me to living in different places and respecting each as if it was our very own. Little did I know then, but that, coupled with the dichos I learned from my mother when I was a child, would be my greatest gifts and lessons in life.

Because of my parents, I lived in some of the most ethnically diverse neighborhoods in this country. I was exposed to many different walks of life, cultures, and problems in each of these communities. But what I experienced most profoundly is the openness and honesty that my family provided to us, our friends, and everyone they met, regardless of ethnicity or economic stature.

I watched my father's never-ending commitment to his dream and his family, while he provided service to others as a physician. To this day he always educates his patients on ways of improving themselves to live longer and healthier lives, never denying service to anyone whether or not they have money or insurance, and taking on the challenges of medical and governmental administrations to give medicine back to the community. I watched my father for over twenty-five years doing this every day, never expecting anything, not even a thank you.

My father's story is what inspired me to pursue my dreams. I watched my mother support my father and our family through those trying times. My mother's story, her legacy, is what motivates and drives me to never give up and continue forward. Her tireless and selfless example has armed me with the most important lessons that I try to live by.

Ironically, as a young woman, it was my beautiful mother who wanted to be a lawyer. But as the eldest daughter, she had to care for her brothers and sisters. She was the backbone of her family and is the backbone of our family. My father's story is truly exceptional and awe inspiring and if it were a movie it would likely win a few prestigious awards. However, my mother would win the Best Director award. Without my mother, my life would not be what it is today.

When I asked my father what he felt was the definition of the American Dream, he replied: "Simple—the opportunity to work, raise and provide for my family, and my children, as well as obtaining the best education possible." He added, "What you can do in this country, you cannot do anywhere else in the world."

Because of them, I am truly living out the American Dream. Through varying circumstances and despite limited options, my parents integrated our culture as a necessary part of this dream. Our culture did not take away from the experience of making it in the United States. On the contrary, it was an equally important and necessary tool to make our assimilation easier.

I believe that within the American Dream culture must continue to thrive. It is vitally important to teach your children to learn, and live by the traditions of your own culture, including, if possible, language. We must be proud of every aspect of our dynamic culture and upbringing. I am constantly told that we (Latinos in general) are the best looking, the best dancers; we have the best cuisine, and can throw one heck of a party. We are likely the loudest on the block, too! Also, we are unique, in that many of us are able to use two languages in one conversation. I am blessed because my first language is Spanish. I learned English around the age of ten. However, I made it my goal to perfect both languages.

My husband is a second-generation Puerto Rican. His parents decided not to teach him Spanish; they felt their children would have better opportunities if English were their dominant language. But does the fact that he does not speak Spanish perfectly make him less Latino or cultureless? In my opinion, no, it does not. In fact, when I first met Christopher I could not believe how passionate he was about the rights of his community. He had the same fire that drove my parents and drives me. He felt indignant over the same injustices toward his people. He made me reflect on my own commitments.

Culture is part of who we are. It makes up our basic essence. My husband and I share so many of the same values, morals, passions, expectations, and experiences. We both love talking, we are people's people. He is loud—sometimes too loud. You name it—family, business, work ethic, friendships, food, we also share many of the same traditions. He can walk into any room and just work it! He is dynamic in a way I can only describe a Latino man to be. I know it is our culture that connects us. It was definitely what attracted us to each other. Well, of course, Christopher is not bad looking either!

As with both of the homes we grew up in, we also expect that our house will be the most crowded with our daughter Sofia's friends. It is funny how that worked out—all of my non-ethnic friends always felt most comfortable in this Latina's house. It must have been the Spanish and I guess a little of the fun, flavor, and food.

I am honored to be asked to speak around the country to my community peers not just on immigration issues, but as in this book, about life experiences. I owe all of this to my upbringing. In comparison to what my parents have conquered, I do not think I have done enough. There is always more to learn and more to do for others.

Today, I am more sure of myself, of my identity, and of my purpose than ever. Yes, I could attribute this to age and experience. But I think it is also in the blood. I always say that I can do anything because *"Tengo la sangre de una mujer latina—*

tengo la sangre de mi madre" (I have the blood of a Latina woman—I have the blood of my mother). So when people ask me: Cristina, how do you do it all? I answer with the most appropriate dicho: *"De tal palo, tal astilla"* (The apple does not fall far from the tree). These few words have been my secret and inspiration for knowing I can succeed at anything I set my mind to. It is the legacy my parents began and one that I will continue.

My Wish for You

This book celebrates culture and my beliefs about a woman's role within it. It is also a celebration of your own culture and your role within it. I will address many questions I am constantly asked, including: How, as a Latina, can you make it in a so-called man's world? How do I win respect in a bilingual world? How am I able to successfully balance a family and career? As a Latina, how have I been able to blend in successfully in the United States? But do not be misled, as this book is for everyone regardless of race, gender, or age.

Today, more than ever, there seems to be a denial of culture among young Latino women and men. Not only does society question who we are, we try to define what it really means to be a Latino in the United States. We try so hard to make it in mainstream America that we forget and sacrifice the very things that make us unique—our culture and identity. We look to others for inspiration and instruction, when we should be looking to ourselves, our parents, our ancestors, and our cultural traditions.

My wish is to teach, guide, and inspire pride in *all people,* especially the younger generation. The key to success is to stay connected to your culture. The answers to all our questions lie within us. As my mother tells me and as I will tell my daughter, *"Lo que bien se aprende, nunca se pierde"* (What is well learned is never lost).

CHAPTER TWO

A Tapestry of Tradition

"Más vale malo conocido, que bueno por conocer"
(Knowing what is bad is better than not knowing at all)

Fascination with a familial patchwork quilt lies in the story of each patch as the quilt is passed along from generation to generation. When the story of the quilt is told, the young listener suddenly realizes that the quilt is so much more than thread and cloth. What they have been gifted with, as my own mother has gifted me, is a deep, personal connection to their heritage and inspiration to continue learning more about their family, culture, and roots.

In this way, dichos are so much more than witty sayings and preachy proverbs. Dating back to the early Spanish settlers of the South American colonies, dichos have been used by Latino families around the world.

Spanish sailors first began settling permanently in Colombia and in Central and South America in the early 1500s. Later in the 1500s, Catholic priests established missions in the Spanish settlements in the Americas to bring Christianity to Native Americans. Therefore, many dichos have roots in the Bible, and the theologians and philosophers of the Catholic Church. Spanish missionaries such as Antonio Montesino (?–1545) and Bartolomé de las Casas (1484–1566) likely brought these words of wisdom to the Americas along with other goods and treasures.

Señor Montesino was best known for publicly denouncing the prevalent Indian slavery, but Bartolomé de las Casas was also known for defending the native Indians, and more famously for revealing the contents of Columbus's diary from his first voyage to the Americas. De las Casas noted in his writings:

> God made all the peoples of this area, many and varied as they are, as open and as innocent as can be imagined . . . Never quarrelsome or belligerent or boisterous, they harbour no grudges and do not seek to settle old scores; indeed, the notions of revenge, rancour and hatred are quite foreign to them . . . They are also among the poorest people on the face of the earth; they own next to nothing and have no urge to acquire material possessions. As a result they are neither ambitious nor greedy, and are totally uninterested in worldly power.

De las Casas's words of humble wisdom, contrasting the modest, simple living of the Indians to the more lavish lifestyles of the Spanish settlers, bring to mind a dicho that is as true today as it was in the 1500s: *"No es más rico el que más tiene, sino el que menos necesita"* (The richest is not the one who has the most, but the one who needs the least). Someone who is satisfied with a small amount is richer than someone who is always craving more.

De las Casas saw that the Native Americans were content with what they had, versus the early Spanish sailors, who seemed obsessed with jewels and acquired wealth. Living by this dicho is important in today's materialistic world. We must seek satisfaction in the wisdom of our culture versus craving what we don't have. If we only search for the material things in life, we risk losing our identity. Be careful because, as another of my favorite dichos states, *"El que todo quiere, todo pierde"* (The one who wants it all loses it all).

Dichos are specific to their country of origin. For instance, since I was raised by Colombian parents and lived for many years in México, the dichos that I grew up with are from Colombia and México. Those early missionaries and colonists may have sewn the first stitch but Latino countries across the globe have made their own dichos, reflecting their specific customs and traditions. The collection of dichos treasured by a country, culture, or community provides a glimpse into the values and belief systems that have guided the group for the length of their existence.

Legendary union organizer and activist Cesar Chavez (1927–93) learned Mexican dichos from his mother such as:

"lo que usted hace a otros, otros le hacen a usted" (what you do to others, others do to you), and *"lleva dos la lucha, uno no puede hacerla sola"* (it takes two to fight, and one can't do it alone). Obviously his mother's lessons had an effect on Chavez when he later coined his chant: *"Sí se puede!"* (Yes, it can be done).

Sandra Cisneros (1954–), America's best-known Mexican-American novelist, uses dichos in her novels as part of her self-described "anti-academic voice . . . the voice of an American-Mexican." An award-winning writer, Cisneros has cleverly used dichos as a lyrical gateway between her two cultures. The author was born in Chicago, the third child in a family of seven. She famously described her motivation to study writing: "I always tell people that I became a writer not because I went to school but because my mother took me to the library. I wanted to become a writer so I could see my name in the card catalog."

Dichos clearly had an impact on Cisneros's life. In the introduction to *My First Book of Proverbs/Mi primer libro de dichos* by Ralfka Gonzalez and Ana Ruiz, Sandra Cisneros wrote: "Dichos will fill you with a wise and foolish laughter."

Cisneros earned a bachelor of arts in English from Loyola University in Chicago and a master's degree in creative writing from the University of Iowa. However, it seems as if much of her wisdom arises from her life experiences. The most valuable lessons learned in life are from living, not from books. What I learned from my parents could have never been received from a university degree.

Another literary legend, among Latinos, the Spanish author Miguel de Cervantes Saavedra (1547–1616), used dichos in the voice of his lead character, Sancho Panza, in his classic, *Don Quixote*. Dichos allowed Cervantes to clearly describe life "in simple, honest and well-measured words."

The dichos that Cervantes chose to communicate with were most likely reflections of his own experience. Starting from a humble upbringing minus a university education, Cervantes's life never contained a dull moment. It included fighting in Turkish battles, being kidnapped by pirates for five years for ransom, and imprisonment for debt, when he started writing his most famous novel. As a result, his characters peppered interesting dichos into their language.

> *"Los bromistas encuentran que son ellos los que están siendo engañados"*
> (Jokers find that they're the ones being fooled)

> *"Ésos a los que se le ha dicho la verdad no se deben de tomar como los que han sido despreciados"*
> (Those who have been told the truth should not be taken for those who have been scorned)

> *"Dime con quién andas, y te diré quién eres"*
> (Say to me with whom you walk and I will say to you who you are)

Don Quixote started with nothing, battled great obstacles, learned from life, and later communicated those lessons through his work. From front porches to front pages and beyond, dichos are firmly grounded in history.

Although they were seemingly worlds apart, Señor Cervantes might have found a close compatriot in Benjamin Franklin. Or, as I affectionately call him, "Señor Dicho." Mostly known for his role as a Founding Father of America, Franklin would often refer to himself as a printer, even signing his name as such.

Here was a man who appreciated the power of language and spent considerable time writing proverbs for his newspapers, almanacs, and other publications. Like dichos, Franklin's famous sayings were written with the intention of offering guidance and Franklin began penning volumes of proverbs as a way of keeping himself moral and productive. However, once he began publishing his "colonial dichos," a new tradition was born. Any of these sound familiar?

> *"Early to bed and early to rise makes a man healthy, wealthy, and wise"*

> *"Never leave that till tomorrow which you can do today"*

> *"In this world nothing can be said to be certain, except death and taxes"*

> *"A penny saved is a penny earned"*

All communication is powerful, but as you can see, dichos and their sister sayings, proverbs, are a special piece of history. A Latino heritage that began with Spanish leaders was personalized inside the home, and then magnified on a grand scale by literary, historical, and religious figures, Latino and non-Latino alike.

The best advice I can give my daughter on how to weave the lessons of our family throughout her life and hopefully throughout future generations is by first learning from both the good and bad of what we've experienced. *"Más vale malo conocido, que bueno por conocer"* (Knowing what is bad is better than not knowing at all). I will tell her and show her by example how knowing what you know and have in your heart is an excellent starting point. She will learn valuable lessons from the life experiences that we've shared with her, but she also has to learn how to experience life on her own.

CHAPTER THREE

Life: Powered by Dichos

"El que no sabe es como el que no ve"
(One who has no knowledge is like one who does not see)

I have a confession to make: I was born in the United States, but because my family lived outside of this country while I was growing up I didn't know a lick of English when we returned to the United States. My dad vividly remembers the cross-border road trip back to the States from Guadalajara. We were all excited about the move, and soon started talking about language issues. My sister and brother knew a little English because they started going to school in the United States, while I started in México.

I knew a few words, but was hardly fluent in English. So of course my brother and sister made fun of me, teasing, "If you

live in the States you need to learn English! They don't speak
Spanish in the States!" They started quizzing me in the car and
somehow arrived at the question of how to say *vaca* (cow) in
English. My dad remembers that after several attempts to remember the translation, I became so frustrated that I finally
just yelled: "Mooo!"

It's amazing that one moment from a seemingly comical
and innocent early childhood experience had an impact on me
for the rest of my life. My father believes that this experience
motivates me today to always go the extra distance. He often
says to me, *"Siempre has sido muy despierta."* (You have always
been very awake.) Not knowing gave me the motivation to
learn. I just hate not knowing.

We all know how difficult rough times can be, and usually
we manage to find our way through them. We're used to it.
For some reason it's easier to make it over a bump in the road
than it is to continuously handle "regular life." It is during
those times when things are going well (or at least status quo)
that you need a solid supply of guidance from your parents,
family, God, or a higher power. During such times, ask yourself: What knowledge do I already have to guide me through
these calm waters? Learn and live by that knowledge, those
traditions, and you will always have a strong boat to weather
any storm.

Knowledge has been the root of power throughout history,
and so it is no accident that knowledge is the root of dichos.
With a little knowledge anything is possible. My favorite and
most treasured dichos were passed down from my mother,
aunts, and grandmothers. I am able to solve various challenges

in life by adhering to their wisdom. I use each dicho to better understand life, enhance my communication with others, and gain more insight into people and their culture. By implementing the dichos my life gains more color, texture, and meaning.

By teaching my daughter the dicho *"El que no sabe es como el que no ve"* (One who has no knowledge is like one who does not see), I want her to know that she only has to open her eyes to see the knowledge in her heart.

I have noticed a funny thing about knowledge and life lessons. For some reason, people keep trying to reinvent the wheel. We believe that the piece of advice that will fix our problems has eluded us. We find ourselves on an endless journey to discover this secret knowledge. I'm here to tell you that we *all* have this knowledge and the power that comes with it. Our parents, relatives, teachers, friends, and a higher power have taught it to us many, many times through words and actions. *"El principio de la sabiduría es trabajar por adquirirla"* (The beginning of knowledge is working to acquire it). My purpose is to help you begin to acquire this knowledge and to use it in your life. Like Dorothy in *The Wizard of Oz,* you've had it all along.

Lessons for Relationships and Marriage

CHAPTER FOUR

Surviving Your Relationships

"A palabras necias, oídos sordos"
(To foolish words, deaf ears)

This dicho should ring true to anyone who has ever successfully survived a relationship. To allow foolish words to fall on deaf ears, like suffering fools gladly, is a necessity for any long-term commitment, particularly marriage. In fact, this is the most important piece of advice my mother gave me for making a marriage work, and I apply it to *all* my relationships. Quite honestly, if I were to hang on to every word that people, including my husband, say to me, I would be crazy!

The phrase "surviving relationships" seems to be an oxymoron. After all, I believe it is human nature to be with another person for a long period of time. Yet, at the same time, it is a huge challenge to commit to one person for a lifetime. It is our nature as human beings to nurture and care for one another. Why, then, is it so difficult for relationships to succeed? Why are relationships, whether business, friendship, or romantic, often emotionally draining? It's for the same reason that anything seems challenging—denial of reality. If the greatest athlete in the world doesn't know the rules of the game, he will fail. Likewise, if we don't understand the basic rules of relationships, we will fail.

On Friendships

"La amistad sincera es un alma repartida en dos cuerpos"
(True friendship is one soul shared by two bodies)

"Hey Pee Wee!" When my father-in-law, Ray Gonzalez, was sick and dying of cancer, his friends the Dukes were right at his side, calling out their friend's childhood nickname. The group had formed when they were thirteen years old, hanging out on the streets of New York City, and when my husband's beloved father passed away, it was the Dukes who carried his coffin at the funeral. They electrified the air with their mere presence, their sadness. From the Irish Duke to the Dominican Duke to the Puerto Rican Duke, Ray was their leader, helping to keep the close knit group together for over fifty years. When he died, a little piece of each of them died, too.

Ray was born in one of the poorest neighborhoods in New York City. His parents were born in Puerto Rico and moved to the United States in the 1930s. Despite his surroundings he excelled in school. In fact, he was accepted into the best private school in the city. However, due to financial circumstances he could not afford to attend and went to a public high school instead.

While growing up he became affiliated with, for lack of a better term, a hodgepodge of friends. There was Ray, the Duke they named Pee Wee (he was short), Whitey (he was the only white guy), Flunky (he had failed out of school), Shadow (he was the only black guy), and many more. At the time, the city was somewhat segregated from city block to city block. Certain ethnic groups lived on certain blocks and crossing the street onto another block could get one in serious trouble. Despite this reality, Ray and his friends united to create a gang known as the Dukes.

The Dukes were like the gangs in *West Side Story* with fewer dance numbers, of course. When they went out on the town it was like mixing both sides of the movie together. They had the humor and the mixture of races and came from all different walks of life.

Like any gang, they fought with other gangs over territory, girls, and dominance. Or just fought to fight. Unlike in *West Side Story* where the brother of a gang leader falls in love with the sister of a rival gang's leader, Ray befriended an Irishman, Sidney (Whitey). They became the best of friends. They were so close that some forty years later he became my husband's godfather (when the concept of being a godfather meant something). The relationship Ray and Sidney had is one many envy, including me. It was the ultimate relationship. I have never seen a straight man have such respect, love, and admiration for another man. It was genuine. It was awesome. It was as if they were related by blood. This explains why my husband is so close to his friends.

As poor kids on the streets, as teenagers decked out at all the New York clubs, through the military service and jobs, moving across the nation, sticking by each other through wives, kids, and grandkids, their friendship was always the Dukes' highest priority. They were a family unto themselves who supported and loved each other. These are men who kissed each other on the mouth with machismo pride. Even when most of the Dukes moved on, Ray was always the catalyst to get everyone back together. They would see each other every weekend and in some cases on a daily basis. At my wedding they made my own father, Darío, an honorary Duke, and to this day they still call my husband, Christopher, "Duke."

Can you imagine such a friendship these days? My advice to you is to go find your own Dukes. Keep them close and never let them go. Unfortunately "friendship counselors" don't exist, so we're basically left on our own to figure it out, but any Duke can tell you that true friendship is an excellent way to value the small and ultimately most important things in life.

"Entre mas amistad, mas claridad"
(The more friends you try to have, the clearer the meaning of friendship becomes)

I tend to always see and believe the good in people. From first impressions onward, when I'm someone's friend I'm his or her friend, case closed. My gut feelings are almost never wrong. Well, at least that's how it used to be, but since I've grown older I've been wrong about people a heck of a lot more often. Why? I've been burned a few times by so-called friends who were not true to their word, feelings, or values. Today friendship is more casual than ever. People say what they think you want to hear and, sadly, at times they're with you just because it's beneficial or convenient for them in some way. I've learned that while optimism is always an admirable trait, you should not be afraid to second-guess a situation when you feel it's wrong in your gut and soul. People can betray you so easily. The most important defense against this is quite simple: Know what you know! Here are some signs that a relationship might not be salvageable.

• Your "friend" stops listening to you. For instance, perhaps you said something to the person one day ago and it's already forgotten. Ever feel like you're talking to a wall?

• The person easily dismisses you. Rejection is palpable in their words and actions. Friends should make you feel important and when they blow you off regularly (everyone is allowed special circumstances, but not all the time), they're not being much of a friend.

• You don't enjoy your friend's company. Friendship should be a source of pleasure, not pain. Dichos give you that type of wisdom as a "sixth sense."

I know that ending any type of relationship sometimes feels like you're throwing in the towel. If you know in your heart that a relationship is not working—you're with a person who doesn't make you feel good about yourself or valuable— then you have no reason to feel guilty about moving on. *"Mejor solo, que mal acompañado"* (It is better to be alone than to be with the wrong person).

Here's the reality of friendships and how to survive and enjoy them: *"Hay que sembrar para recoger"* (You have to sow to reap). You can't realistically expect a friendship to last simply because you've known someone since high school. Friendships take work—you can't expect your friends will always be there, yet never call them or give them a second thought without a specific reason, such as needing something from them. If you treated your marriage or romantic relationships like that, how long do you think they would last? Not long before fizzling out! It takes "two to tango" in any relationship. That's why it amazes me how people ignore their friends and take them for granted, yet seriously expect them to be "on standby" forever. I must admit that I too am guilty of being that kind of friend and struggle with it all the time. It's not a dicho per se, but have you heard the phrase "out of sight, out of mind"? You cannot just pretend something into reality. We are told to work on our marriage. I'm here to tell you that *all* relationships require effort, communication, maintenance, and nurturing—at home, at work, and everywhere in between.

Workplace Relationships

"Con virtud y bondad se adquiere autoridad"
(With virtue and goodness authority is acquired)

I model my business relationships after those that I've admired over the years. In business, especially law firms, people are always trying to get into partnerships and alliances as a sign of prestige, but I have a friend who is not afraid to go against the tide and prides himself on having worked his whole life *not* to have a law partner. I admire that kind of independence. Although, based on that thinking, you might think that working on good relationships with his staff would not be his top priority, but it's exactly the opposite. He is honest and upfront with the associates from the beginning and tells them that they will never be a partner. He grows his staff, teaches them to be great lawyers, and then sends them out on their own, like his kids, to realize their own success.

What is remarkable and also perhaps unusual in such a competitive world is that my friend is never threatened by the potential success of his employees. He does not worry that they might be better than he is. That kind of paranoid thinking comes from a place of low self-confidence that is simply not in this gentleman's nature. The fact that he is not threatened by his protégés makes for a healthy relationship based on mutual respect and admiration. He takes pride in his protégés' success and, because of that, I am proud to call him my friend.

Closer to home, my father is even more of a personal relationship role model for me. He has such good and honest relationships with his patients that they can really trust him with complicated issues. His personal connection with his patients gives them the security that someone is listening to them. I take pride in emulating him when I do business with my clients.

"De la abundancia del corazón, habla la boca" is a dicho that means "from the abundance of your heart, your mouth speaks." That's exactly how business relationships should be approached, with riches coming from the heart, as I learned from my father's example.

For all the time I've spent in the workplace, from my very first job until now as owner of my law firm, I have always been myself. This courage to be myself, under all circumstances and in all situations, has a lot to do with the success and happiness I have achieved throughout my career. I have talked about the example set by my father as a role model and guide in all aspects of my life, and I attribute so much of my success to following his blueprint, by maintaining my personality and identity.

My first job as an attorney was in an office of all women and two men, both of whom were my bosses. Although I was an associate attorney, I wasn't afraid to play the nurturing role of a woman. I wasn't doing it consciously—it was what my mother taught. I did everything from making coffee to caring for my co-workers ("my kids"). At first the ladies in the office had a hard time with me, the confused feminist that I am, practicing law and being an office mom at the same time, but eventually they realized that this wasn't an act. I wasn't doing it to send a message. I was just being myself.

People often do exactly the opposite. They don't act like themselves at all. Instead, they try to prove some kind of point. People simultaneously fear and crave competition and may self-destruct in the face of it. I have found that welcoming competition while respecting my competitors has made all my workplace experiences more enjoyable, productive, and rewarding.

On a smaller, more realistic scale, away from the dark side of office politics, it's the simple things, like taking the time to say hello, please, or thank you that make all the difference. Sometimes I wonder if people's mothers taught them about manners! Co-workers forget their manners while trying to be something they're not, which often leads to conflict. At the root of this is the misconception that accepting each other as naturally nurturing human beings is somehow demeaning. These behaviors are not demeaning, they are respectful. Be who you are, all aspects at the same time. Yes, it's true that you should separate business and pleasure. But you should also bring some piece of yourself to your work at all times. It is important to appreciate the work being done in the office, and the people doing the work, starting with yourself. Believe me, balancing a love of healthy competition, respect for your co-workers, good manners, and above all, being yourself at all times, will make for a much better day at the office.

QUICK TIP

Say "thank you":

Buy thank you cards and use them liberally. Strive to write a quick note to a friend, co-worker, or colleague once a week or once a month expressing why your relationship is valuable to you. Also, don't be stingy with your compliments. They only take a second and will surely brighten someone's day.

CHAPTER FIVE

Maintaining a Marriage

"El matrimonio es un mal necesario"
(Marriage is a necessary evil)

The institution of marriage is based on S&M. I'm not trying to be kinky here, but it's true. Women are masochists at heart. We are harder on ourselves than anyone else could possibly be, and frequently put ourselves last, after our marriage, kids, and work. And don't try to convince us otherwise or we'll launch into a massive guilt trip that could last for years, ruining the lives of everyone around us! Men, on the other hand, are sadists. Why blame yourself when there are so many other available targets right in front of you? Of course I'm kidding, but this sheds some light on the overall formula of marriage. A guilt-ridden woman plus a footloose and fancy free man equals the tendency of both partners to perceive that marriage is, indeed, a necessary evil and often requires as much maintenance as a Boeing 747.

I certainly do not think that marriage is evil. However, like anything else truly rewarding and wonderful, it requires a lot of work. An unwritten truth of life is you can't have it both ways. At some point most people want to get married and will. Once you are married ask yourself: What are you doing to maintain your marriage? After all, you wanted it so badly! Remember the butterflies leading up to your Cinderella wedding? You just couldn't wait to get that ring on your finger. Well, it's not over after that. The key to true love is maintenance.

"El matrimonio no es sólo para un día" (Marriage is not only for a day). Just because you get married doesn't mean you're set for life. The honeymoon is really over if you forget that you are married. It took many years to find this person and now it's going to take a lifetime commitment to maintain your *new* relationship with them, your marriage. It's not the end of a marathon just because you have your cute little titles—"Mr. and Mrs."—and some pretty little rings. It takes work every day, all the time.

Why did older generations, such as my parents, have such successful marriages? Why is it that they knew how to keep a marriage and we don't? When we were being raised, did we misunderstand something, or were we never taught the value of a family unit? Marriage is a difficult responsibility, but once we enter into the sacred bonds of marriage, it is our obligation to work hard at maintaining it. This reminds me of another favorite dicho, *"Casamiento y mortaja, del cielo bajan"* (Marriage, like death, is already chosen for you). Don't look for it, and don't rush it. It will eventually happen for you and when it does, consider it a blessing, sometimes in disguise.

The greatest blessing in a marriage, of course, is your spouse (this includes husband, wife, or partner), as supported by another of my mother's favorite sayings—*"La prioridad del matrimonio es el esposo o la esposa"* (The top priority of a marriage is your spouse). I'm not saying that your children aren't extremely important, but once you have raised them and they leave the house, whom are you left with? You're left with the person that you married. And if you didn't work to maintain and nurture your relationship for all the years of your marriage, your relationship is going to be in real trouble once the nest is empty. This is an especially delicate balancing act for women, God's natural-born nurturers. Sure, in a way, it's kind of a selfish thing to admit that your spouse is more important, but remember that your husband or wife is your life partner. Your children are going to leave and start their own lives, leaving you to continue on with your life as a couple. It's your job to make sure that there is still a life to be led.

Sex

"Del agua mansa me libre Dios, que de la brava me libro yo"
(May God deliver me from meek waters, for I will stay away
from the turbulent ones)

I often joke that "men only want food, sex, and silence!" Seriously, one must be very alert in life to survive all the elements of a marriage—from meek to rough waters. We find ourselves in meek waters when we're not alert and doing the work it takes to maintain a marriage. That is when things begin to fizzle out and need to be reignited. Remember that honesty and communication make up the foundation of every relationship, especially marriage. If we cannot be honest and confide in our spouses, who else can we really trust? Sex is also an important aspect in every relationship. It contains a level of intimacy and connection that supersedes words.

With this said, intimacy and passion should always be present in a relationship. Every relationship at the beginning is riddled with that "can't keep your hands off each other" passion, and that "butterflies in your stomach" feeling. With marriage comes responsibility, children, and working. It is natural for sex to take a back seat for a bit. But it should not disappear! It is our responsibility to make sure these feelings do not fade away. It takes work and effort. Why is it that we get married and forget to have sex? We cannot wait for our partners to make the first move. You make the first move! Create a special romantic night with your spouse. Confide in him and tell him you miss those initial feelings, that you miss *him*, and want to reignite the feelings. You may be surprised—he may be feeling the same way.

I will now address the more serious topic of a chronically sexless marriage woman to woman *(de mujer a mujer)*. It happens to more people than you know. This is sometimes a normal phase that occurs in many marriages, but only to a degree. As the saying goes: *"Estoy como el recién casado, con ganas de mucho y sin ganas de nada"* (I feel like a newlywed, yearning greatly and wanting nothing). This doesn't just apply to new-lyweds, either. A sexless marriage can easily occur when a couple becomes complacent. You become so busy with life that you forget to face your problems because neither of you wants to push the issue and risk escalating it into something worse.

These truly are the meek waters, when you're in danger yet convince yourself that it's really okay, all because you don't want to be the one to say anything and rock the boat. These are the waters you need to be careful of because therein lies the danger of living within the problem until finally it is too late to be solved. The initial danger period comes and goes and you think that the problem is "real life" getting in the way of your relationship and you become complacent. Does any of this sound familiar? "I have something else to do"; "Next month when things aren't so hectic"; or "Maybe when we take that vacation and I'm more relaxed."

I'll admit that some of this applies to me. I'm mad that I sometimes let real life get in the way of one of the most valuable relationships I have. I'm denying myself something I enjoy doing! I tell myself, "He has to understand how exhausted I am." Does he really? Convincing yourself of something like that is a type of complacency that comes from assumptions that are just plain wrong. He doesn't know! How could he if you don't muster the courage to tell him how you're feeling? You may have fooled yourself but you can't fool your marriage.

Beware of the danger of monotony in a relationship. It's a crisis that needs to be handled. What may seem like an innocent loss of libido could easily lead to loss of love in a marriage. And yes, men, this goes both ways. If you explore the situation, and determine that one or both of you just does not like sex and you do not want to make love, there is a bigger problem than can be solved by this book. I suggest you speak to your wife or husband and then both of you see a therapist. Living like this is not fair to either of you, and is certainly not fair to your marriage and the commitment you've made to each other.

Marital Advice

*"Cuando te cases acuérdate de tratar
a tu esposo como un esposo. No trates de ser su mamá.
El ya tiene una"*
(When you marry remember to treat your husband like a
husband. Do not try to be his mother—he already has one)

This was the best advice my mother gave me on marriage and maintaining my relationship with my husband. It is an important point, as the tendency is the exact opposite. What is it about women that we are so demanding with our husbands? We order them around all the time as if we really are their mothers! Our need to have things done "now" causes such problems. I ask my husband to do something and literally give him one second to do it before asking him again. Every time I do it I want to kick myself. As the book says, men and women really are from different planets.

Are women perfectionists or controllers? It seems as if subconsciously we need to dictate and control everything. In some ways we are altogether too demanding and expect far too much from our husbands. In our defense, we do have more responsibility in life at home, work, and everywhere in between. Another theory perhaps goes back to the beginning of time when a family's shelf life depended on how quickly the cave husband made it back home with food for the wife and kids. Is nagging programmed into our female hormones as a survival mechanism? If so, I often joke that the ferocity of the urge should be weakening from generation to generation, so there's a chance that our granddaughters might be less prone to do it.

When a woman behaves like this, the relationship deteriorates. The behavior also leads to a loss of intimacy between a husband and wife. We must find the balance between being our husband's wife and being his mother because when we get married, we are only his spouse.

Overcoming such tendencies and maintaining a successful marriage is simply a matter of understanding and accepting one's role in the relationship. There is something to be said about giving a little to get a lot in return.

If things are not going smoothly, yes, it is easy to quit. But is that what you promised your spouse when you got married? The most common complaints I hear about marriage from my friends and even myself and my husband, are that "she is always nagging"; "he just doesn't listen"; and "we are always arguing." While I believe it is healthy to express yourself freely without fear of repercussion (free expression is part of any healthy relationship), there are boundaries. This expression should not be abused or used as a form of manipulation. You also need to know when to stop and when to let go. Most important, always listen!

The key to maintaining a successful marriage is having a good friendship with your partner. A strong friendship with solid communication is paramount. My husband and I have developed a wonderful friendship. We allow ourselves the right to our opinions, and maybe because we are both lawyers, we argue. No, let me rephrase that. We cross-examine each other, with any and every legal strategy each of us has learned in our years of practice. In the midst of these "interrogations," I remember my mother's advice. Which advice? All of her advice! Remember the dicho about foolish words falling on deaf ears? After all, which advice from *your* mother are you willing to toss to the side? So, during those "courtroom battles" with my husband, I am careful to follow my mother's advice, object to the questioning, and, well, either walk out of the room or just laugh.

I've noticed over the years that what used to be fifteen-minute arguments now take only thirty seconds. In a marriage you must learn to be more selective about the things you fight for or you'll lose your sanity. Sure, my husband and I have disagreements, but we know our separate roles—mine is that of a traditional woman. Sometimes I'm at home, exhausted from a full day of work, and yet I'm still cooking dinner for my husband and momentarily wondering why. Accepting my role doesn't mean I can't nag once in a while! I'm still human, after all. But I know it will take more energy to change things. My mother says, *"El que se casa, casa quiere,"* which means that if you get married you take on all the responsibilities of a home and a marriage.

Marriage requires that partners communicate and give each other space to grow as separate individuals. Remember, you married people who were people before they married you, who loved to do things. Maybe they played golf, liked to shop, or played chess. They had a life before you!

Yes, when you get married there's a responsibility to your partner, but I think it's cruel when one spouse doesn't let the other continue doing the things they are passionate about. Let your spouses continue expressing their personalities. This will only make the relationship stronger.

Some time alone is necessary for personal growth. I am not saying to go on separate vacations, but to give each other allotted days to enjoy a hobby or whatever your partner likes to do. Please remind me of this when I get upset at my husband for golfing whenever he gets the chance!

My husband loves to play golf and hits the links on a regular basis. I certainly can't complain about it. I recognize that I am Christopher's true golf widow. Golf was there before me. My mother always tells me, *"¿Porque te quejas, si sabes dónde está todo el tiempo?"* (Why are you complaining? At least you know exactly where he is at all times!) Because even when he's golfing, my husband calls me three or four times during the game, to the point where, unlike the typical wife, I'm saying, "Leave me alone! You're doing your own thing and I'm doing mine." Giving each other space and independence gives the relationship a new life. Maintaining your individual identities maintains the marriage. If you are not happy with yourself, how can you be happy in a marriage?

It is also important to keep the romance alive. Pick and

stick to a day or a time dedicated only to each other. Have a date night, something special. It's important to balance the dramatic "sweep you off your feet" romance (the rose petals, tropical getaways and such) with the everyday things. My mother always says, *"La vida esta llena de detalles,"* which means "Life is full of details." It's the little details that count the most and are par for the course, not the big sweeping gestures and certainly not the giant diamonds! Even though I also need space, it's the phone calls from the golf course that score the highest points in my book.

Responsibility

"Si quieres el perro, acepta las pulgas"
(If you want the dog you must accept the fleas)

In a marriage there is always going to be one person who has more responsibility. Sometimes it may be the man and other times the woman, but you need to accept that this is your marriage's unique blueprint and learn to appreciate it. If you happen to be the one carrying more of the workload (such as responsibilities with the house, kids, bills) it obviously takes patience and understanding to exist peacefully in your role. Sometimes when I'm overwhelmed I tell Christopher, "I'm the one with more on my plate—help me out!" because it's true and he knows it. I don't say this to blame him or out of frustration, because really it's my problem. I know I have more to do at home and my husband understands that and helps as much as he can. Once again, it comes back to know-ing your role on the "team" (in my case, owner, manager, quarterback, and waterboy!) and accepting it with honesty and patience.

I may sound like a confused feminist but in accepting the role of traditional wife and mother, by no means am I being submissive or taking away from my role as a successful woman with a career in law and on television. I am just accepting my part of the marriage. I am not just giving in. There are things in life that you need to accept. If women understood this they would have fewer problems overall. I prefer to make it easy for my husband because that's how my mother treats my father to this day. It's really quite beauti-ful—she tends to him and caters to him in a traditional sense. But out of respect, my father and Christopher will not abuse a woman's caring. Without this respect, it would be much easier to see our actions as submissive when in reality they are rooted in love. Taking care of the people you love should never be seen as subservient.

Don't try to be a flat character just because society wants to stereotype women as either career feminists or traditional homemakers. There is no reason why women can't be both. Why does society try to make everyone a flat character and then complain that we have no depth as a society? My con-fused feminism may confuse others, but for me, it's the only way to maintain my marriage and live my life. Christopher and I don't have a perfect marriage—nobody does. What I've learned is that I do have the perfect partner for me. That is the most any of us can ever ask for. As my mother always says and

I will teach my daughter, *"Ahí esta el amor, en las buenas y en las malas"* (Love is present in good and bad times).

QUICK TIP

Take time to talk to your spouse/partner. Look them in the eye, ask them about their day, and *pay attention*.

CHAPTER SIX

Crisis Management

"El amor es el vino, que mas presto se avinagra"
(Love is like wine, it sours quickly)

I am a passionate wine lover! *Vino* is meant to be opened, and enjoyed with peace and satisfaction. It takes such an elaborate and specific process to create a good bottle of wine, from the growing and nurturing of hand-selected grapes to plucking them off the vines at exactly the right time. Therefore, when you open a perfectly aged bottle of red wine and forget to drink it in time, and it quickly sours—*¡Qué pesar!*

Like that bottle of wine, it takes so much time, energy, patience, and "fermenting" to get a marriage to a certain place. Why then would anyone endure such efforts to only neglect the marriage?

Surviving Marital Challenges

"Al mal tiempo, buena cara"
(In bad times put on a good face)

In marriage there are going to be things that you cannot control, and usually they are the insignificant things. After all, who said marriage would be easy? Marriage is work and a lot of sacrifice. It is two people with different likes, dislikes, ideas, and customs creating a new and unified life together. My mother is right. Marriage takes friendship, communication, love, respect, faith, trust, passion, and a lot of patience!

For anything worth having, such as a good marriage, there are challenges to overcome. The constantly changing roles of men and women pose one of these challenges. Today's husband is more often needed at home to help raise children, in addition to his more traditional breadwinner duties. Women may find it especially difficult to balance their roles as mother, wife, and professional. Some wives even become resentful toward their husbands if they gave up their profession (even if it was by choice) to be full-time wives and mothers. Admittedly, these are issues our parents might not have had to contend with. That doesn't mean we have an excuse to give up more easily. No, we need to work even harder.

Any relationship is two people coming together with two sets of different likes, dislikes, and cultures. It would be really easy to see those as obstacles, but why not instead see them as reasons to form a closer bond and expand the boundaries of our own reality?

Yes, we live in a fast-paced world. That is a given. Attention spans can be short, while "till death do us part" may be perceived as longer than ever. It can be difficult to live with someone for a long time without getting easily bored and risking the danger of taking the other for granted by focusing on your fast-paced life. It's easy to confuse our priorities while getting caught up in the new and exciting things outside of the house, rather than putting forth the effort needed to keep things alive inside. As the dicho says, *"Amor no se echa en la olla"* (You can't throw love aside when things aren't going your way).

Older generations knew that marriage cannot be bought and sold. They were taught to choose love, stay with the relationship, and never give up. Conversely, our "I want it yesterday!" generations have been taught by society that there is always something better. For our own sake, it's time to slow down. If we start comparing our relationships with the latest and greatest technology, new careers, and cars, then the institution of marriage will never be the same.

I am not suggesting that we turn back the hands of time. That is unrealistic. It is, however, our responsibility to do everything possible to build and maintain strong bonds to ensure that the values we pass along are good ones. I hope my daughter will always choose words that make the most difference in her own life and the lives of those closest to her.

"El que todo lo quiere, todo lo pierde"
(The one who wants it all loses it all)

My biggest marital challenge occurred before I even married Christopher. We met in 1991 and dated six years before marrying. During that time, Christopher never said "I love you" even once to me, which, for most women, would have been a deal breaker. I, however, was the logical one. The lawyer in me was very practical about the situation. During the time we were dating I had met his parents and I knew without a shadow of a doubt that we were exclusive, and had no doubt that I was the only one he was seeing and vice versa. That was not the issue. I knew I loved him. However, I'm a firm believer that love needs to go two ways. One person (me) can be infatuated and have deep feelings, but you can't have true love until both people feel the same way. Logically I said to myself, "I like this guy, but how do I know if I love him?" I knew we cared about each other but we had never said those three special words to each other.

So I went to Christopher and said, "I know we're committed to each other, but I need to understand how we feel about each other. Are we in love?" Suddenly I was his therapist! He responded, "I don't know." I believed him, and said, "You're my friend and I care about you, but I need to know where this is going." I wasn't particularly ready for marriage, but I did not want to give more time to a relationship that wasn't going to last. Being the logical one, I told him, "You need to think about it; I need to think about it, so let's have some time apart. Maybe there's too much on our plates. Let's save our time and energy." Christopher was shocked. I certainly didn't have an ultimatum or ulterior motive for him to come running back, shouting, "I love you, I need you!" I was just being logical.

A couple of days later, Christopher called. "I know I love you and I need you." My initial reaction was "What happened to Christopher and who are you?" Being a lawyer, I cross-examined him. I used an acronym that they teach in law school called IRAC: Issue, rule, analysis, and conclusion. I told him, "The only reason you're saying this is because I brought it up a few days ago." In other words, this wasn't his idea, so how could he possibly believe it? I concluded, "I understand what you're telling me and I believe you, but I think we still need some time to think about it on our own." Sometimes you only want what you can't have. I really wanted to make sure that wasn't the reason behind what he was saying. Was it love or his feelings of rejection? Christopher was devastated and told his father, "She broke up with me!" Years later I learned that his father, Ray, agreed with me in the sense that his son was foolish in risking his love and feelings for what he thought was the responsible thing to do.

Christopher wrote me an incredible letter that laid out his feelings and explained why he was afraid to express his true feelings for me. It turned out that he *was* like many men. He was holding back his feelings the whole time because he felt he needed to be stable—earning an income with a good job to support me. He thought he had to measure up to the same standards as my parents from a monetary standpoint. I pointed out to him that I also was going to law school, and would be going to work, too. The irony here, of course, is that he had more money than my parents did when they got married. Christopher chose to compare his financial situation then with theirs now—like apples and tree bark! A true gentleman, he was in doubt as to whether he could provide for me. In his mind, there was a financial stability issue related to those three powerful little words: "I love you."

Of course, as is always the case in matters of the heart, Christopher also had a more personal and less financially responsible fear of saying "I love you" to me. In his words, he had been "burned" by a relationship in college in which the girl married his college roommate.

So after my IRAC cross-examination and breakup with him, Christopher said, in his words, "I felt like an idiot. I was convinced that you were dating other people . . . I couldn't work, couldn't sleep, and I kept calling your answering machine and hanging up." This was a complete surprise to me, by the way. I had no caller ID back then and I'll admit that I just never put two and two together. How sweet—*¡Qué lindo!* After sending me the heartfelt letter, and a few months of uncertainty, Christopher returned, not being his usual macho self, pleading for me to take him back. My logical response to this was, "Can't you just be normal again?" I was actually very excited because it reaffirmed my gut feeling that we were right for each other, and I'm glad I did what I did.

The overall challenge was overcoming stereotypes. We were living within everyone else's opinions, without being true to ourselves. There was no reason for him not to tell me he loved me just because he didn't have a job. Or for that matter there was no reason for me to wait to tell him, "Hey, I think I love you," until he said it first. He was afraid I didn't feel the same way. The challenge for me was to be satisfied with the way things were. I learned—I think we both learned—that sometimes you have to go through a challenge and risk something in order to gain something even greater. Looking back on the situation, I figured, "If I don't say something now, I'm going to risk the ideal opportunity of my life to meet people or find true love—which ended up being with Chris."

A few months later, we got back together, and it was a *completely* different relationship. Now we knew where the other stood! We had challenged each other to be honest.

He now recalls how our relationship changed significantly after we got back together. "What do I have to lose now?" he thought. He jokes that once I was back by his side, he never again lost golf tournaments, and enjoyed free dinners at my family's house and a great friendship with my parents, particularly my father, his frequent golfing partner (one of the primary reasons for my father's angst when Christopher and I temporarily separated).

From this experience, my advice to you is to challenge yourself to be honest and identify the problem of the relationship. Be true to yourself. Sure, it's easier to be quiet. If you don't ask the hard questions, how are you going to know the truth?

"El que todo lo quiere, todo lo pierde" (The one who wants it all loses it all). While I was left wondering about his intentions and logically questioning "what's love got to do with

it?" he was desperately trying to pull together everything he believed he needed to utter those three magic words: a house, a stable job, and a bank account. He wanted it all and for a brief period of time he lost it all. Thank goodness for my family's persistence—"Where is Christopher? What did you do to him? Where did he go?" I'm also thankful for Christopher's persistence, without which I would have lost one of the greatest blessings of my life and a few years after that, the other blessing of my life—our beautiful little daughter, Sofia Daniella. Yes, there are challenges in every relationship. But if you get real with yourself and with the other person, communicate, and connect, almost every challenge can be overcome. Trust me, the rewards are far worth the trouble!

"El que da primero, da dos veces"
(He who strikes first strikes twice)

There is no such thing as a fair fight, especially when it's personal. Everything outside of an actual boxing ring is personal, particularly in the treacherous relationship arena. Therefore, in a marital argument, the first to throw an insult in a fight hits the hardest. When you strike first with an insult, you are putting your spouse against the ropes and they must now spend the rest of the argument defending themselves and struggling to stand up again. It is never fifty-fifty so why would you want to put your spouse in that position? There is no argument here. An insult is simply an attack on the person you love. It is healthy to argue if that's what you are doing—two people disagreeing. But if the conflict starts with an insult, then it's an attack. Why would you do that to someone who is supposed to be on your team?

One of the most hurtful things you can say to your spouse is "shut up." The irony is that people say "shut up" about minor little nothings, almost casually. There is nothing casual about those two harsh words, which invalidate your spouse's opinion and self-worth. This is the person you married and are in love with. As much as you may think that the words don't matter, they do. Your job is to be the one person in the world who would never invalidate your husband or wife. By demeaning them, you are emotionally abandoning them. Remember to be on their side. Everything you do in a marriage should be a team effort. Understand that we are all human and we all make mistakes, and if we sweat the small stuff it will only lead to bigger stuff.

On the occasions when you do slip up and fight with your partner, you must learn to forgive and forget. *"Perdonar es divino"* means "To forgive is divine." Try not to blame or bring up past mistakes under any circumstances with your spouse. Always forgive each other regardless of who thinks they won. If you really forgive someone, then you forget the fight—it's as if it never existed. True forgiveness is really forgetting. Forgiveness makes you and your marriage stronger.

This next part is embarrassing for me to admit, because I love my husband. Once, we had a really bad fight. The pettiness of that fight alone makes me ashamed. On top of that, I actually threatened Christopher with divorce, and said, "Why don't you just leave?" He responded, "If you want me to I will!" I realized how much I had hurt him. To see the devastation in his eyes taught me to think twice before I do or say anything like that ever again. How could I use the word "divorce" with my husband? Was I just trying to win the fight? What stupidity! The bottom line was that I had hurt someone I love in a fight, and that was the worst feeling in the world for me.

When two people who love each other argue, nobody wins. Especially since the biggest fights seem to be over the smallest, most stupid things. It's absolutely never worth it. A marriage is far too valuable to risk over such garbage. I know that it's the hardest thing in the world to really hold yourself back when you're hurt or angry but regain your focus and remember who the person is in front of you.

When you argue it is so easy to let yourself get carried away. I often tell my husband, *"El que tiene boca se equivoca"* (He who has a mouth will surely make a mistake). For instance, Christopher has a macho New York Puerto Rican quick and dry way of communicating. It's just how he is. Even though he is not trying to be rude, he sometimes sounds that way. At times he argues with me in a very condescending way. I could easily turn around and attack, turning a little argument into a big war. It is much easier for me to ignore it, let it go, while listening and trying to comprehend his point of view. That's the key in times of crisis. Sift through the salt, pepper, and dressing and figure out what the other person is really saying. Wait for the moment to pass and then take up the core issue at a later time, without actually referring to the fight itself.

For example, if your husband gets angry and says something in public that offends you, later on let him know tactfully that you don't appreciate being talked to like that in public (or private for that matter). This is always the better choice for me because Christopher is my husband, and I love him. I chose him to marry and we have built a life with each other. By hearing his real words and not escalating the argument, it completely deflates him, whether he's right or wrong. Christopher has come to know that when I don't argue back, it's either because his argument or point of view is foolish. This has become a great tool for me—possibly even more valuable than IRAC! With just one look he knows what he has done.

Life is too short to let foolish words get to you. So next time you argue with your partner remember my mother's dicho: *"A palabras necias, oídos sordos"* (To foolish words, deaf ears).

Be honest with yourself. Which path do you believe, in your heart of hearts, will what you're about to say or do, propel you down? Is it fair to you? Is it fair to your spouse? Is it fair to your children? Most important, is this what you really want for your marriage? Never forget that you're married and made a commitment to live together and make one another happy. Nobody forced you to get married. You made this choice and you must hold yourself accountable for it. I hope you understand that there are exceptions. Some marriages are not good and there are reasons why people are not meant to be together (such as violence or continued infidelity). But I'm talking about those marriages that are fundamentally good and have a strong foundation. The people are good, but they just let life get to them and need a way to stay together through the rough waters.

To Divorce or Not to Divorce

"Antes que te cases, mira lo que haces"
(Think twice before you marry)

In the Latino culture matrimony is sacred. It has always been that way, still is, and hopefully always will be. Our culture has always taught us that you fall in love, get married, and take your vows of respect and fidelity for the rest of your life. My mother tells me, "Remember, *mija,* for us this is a sacred vow. In any marriage, *el amor*—love, mutual respect, understanding, and patience—is key in maintaining a stable relationship." On the subject of divorce, she says, "Divorce in my time, my parents' time, was just unheard of. You worked on every problem you had because marriage was sacred. Nowadays people get married because they just want to get married, not because it's sacred love or because they want the sacred formation of a family. Maybe that's the sad part."

When I wondered if I had what it takes to honor such a sacred tradition, my mother said to me, "Do you remember before you got married what Father Alden said to you?" I did. Right before we got married, during our pre-wedding interview, the first thing our Catholic priest asked Christopher and me was, "How long have your parents been married?" We answered that both sets of parents had been married thirty-five-plus years. Father Alden responded, "That's it. We're done." We were surprised, since we knew that the purpose of this interview was to make sure we, as the soon-to-be-married couple, understood the importance of marriage and knew how sacred it was. Instead, the priest said, "You guys are fine. You already have a solid foundation for understanding what marriage is. You've seen your parents struggle, and still keep up their marriage, right? You're all set, then." He was absolutely right. I had these values instilled within me and I knew what marriage was going to be like. I had the foundation I needed to maintain my marriage.

What makes some couples more likely to stay together in times of crisis and others flee to divorce court with barely a second thought? The decision to end a marriage lies in the layers of beliefs and values possessed by the husband and wife as individuals.

Think of your belief system as an onion. The outer layer is what you think you know to be true in life because of what you've learned and decided for yourself ("I don't believe in divorce because I wouldn't want to do that to my kids."). Below that, one layer closer to the core, are the morals and values that you have learned directly from your family and relatives ("My parents got divorced and I don't want to go through that"). The next layer contains your religious beliefs and anything else learned from a higher power ("The pastor said till death do us part and I believe that anything else goes against God's wishes"). The core of your beliefs, the "center of the onion," is where the majority of your actions originate from.

This is your own center of the earth. Everything you have ever learned, believed, and absorbed while growing up by observing your parents and loved ones exists at this core.

All of our decisions in times of crisis (marital or otherwise) originate from the human fight or flight syndrome. Basically, this means that when the you-know-what hits the fan, a chemical called adrenaline kicks in and we instinctively choose to stay and fight, or our instincts tell us to flee the situation. Understanding whether your natural tendency is to fight or flee can help give you perspective in a crisis situation before you make a mistake and lose something as precious as your marriage. If instinct is telling you to flee, understand and accept that. Then, take a deep breath and think about what you are about to flee from. This is your marriage.

There must be a larger purpose, a personal purpose, often unrelated to your partner or the marriage itself. Find something in your core that makes you want to honor your commitment, work through the crisis, and make your marriage stronger than ever. For me, I don't give up on marriage because I love my husband and he is my best friend. I cannot see myself with anybody else. He is such a strong, vital part of me. How could I not be with him tomorrow or ten years from now? I'm going to take care of this important piece of me just like I take care of the other parts. I learned from my parents that marriage is really all about connecting my husband to my entire being, and not just seeing him as this person I come home to every night. He is not a separate entity.

Every person is different, but look at the examples you have in your own life—your parents, grandparents, close friends, and others. The Latino culture in itself is an example to draw strength from. You must find a deeper reason to stay in one of the strongest connections offered to us in life.

QUICK TIP

Say "I'm sorry":
Just say it. It doesn't matter who started the fight or who wronged whom. The sooner you apologize, the sooner the argument will end; then you can fix the problem instead of fighting about it.

Lessons for Family and Parenthood

CHAPTER SEVEN

A Solid Foundation

"A los hijos se les tiene que criar con mano de hierro y guantes de seda y hay que criarlos con mucho amor, si no, no les enseñamos nada"
(You must raise your children with hands of steel and with silk gloves and you must raise them with love because without love you will teach them nothing)

Kids today can easily be influenced by everything around them. If they are not connected to the moral compass and guidance of their family, they are essentially "unplugged" from the most important aspects of life. *"Árbol que crece torcido, nunca se endereza"* (A tree born crooked never straightens). Childrearing is especially important in the early years because that's when the foundation of your child's personality is set. During this time you are plugging them into a connection that they will come back to over and over again for the rest of their lives.

Children can be swept up by virtually anything or anyone who comes along. When they're not connected to a greater purpose in life, they are disconnected from logic and common sense, two of life's most valuable assets, and this can best be provided by a child's parents.

Casualness

"Como se vive, se muere"

(How you live is how you are remembered when you die)

My mom always explains to me that you have to take advantage of everything in life and not take anything for granted. Nothing is casual in life except maybe the way you stroll down the street on a spring day. Yet I have observed in newer generations an alarmingly casual attitude about the most important things in life—relationships, marriage, family, and parenting. It's no accident that political and societal trends in the last few decades have begun to reflect that casual attitude.

On my TV show, at work, and in real life, I have observed young people casually deriding their family ("I *have* to spend Thanksgiving with my family—ugh!"), their marriage ("Oh well, I can always get divorced if this doesn't work out"), and worst of all, their children ("I don't want to watch him, you watch him"). We have somehow forgotten that these are the *most* important things in life, not the *least* important. If we do not value these, we will not value anything else in life—right instead of wrong, respect for others, work ethics, and all of those other wonderful "little" things that keep the world moving smoothly.

My mother and father taught me that everything has a meaning and a purpose. You have to be thankful for the journey, even if it is sometimes boring. There is a reason for everything that happens. By believing that, you create forward momentum in your life, learning and improving yourself with every mistake, and accelerating with every victory and milestone.

Children's relationships with their parents are important, especially with their mothers. I have an unusually close relationship with my mother and father—particularly with my mother. I tell her everything—she's my best friend. It's almost crazy how close we are and people may think it's unhealthy. Well, I think the relationship I have with them is priceless. I can count on my parents because they're always there. That kind of unwavering dependability and safety is a constant comfort that all children deserve to have. Culturally for Latinos, having a good relationship with your mother is key. In my world, I have expanded that relationship into an essential friendship that I rely on all the time.

One of the most important aspects of our relationship, is knowing one's role. My parents know how to be my parents, firm, loving, and guiding, and also how to be my friends, but they keep a boundary between those two relationships. They know their roles and I know mine.

"El que no oye consejos, no llega a viejo"
(Those who refuse advice will not mature)

My father once told me, "There are two stages in life—before the age of thirty and after." Before thirty, most children pay little attention to the wisdom their parents are desperately trying to pass along to them. Suddenly, after the age of thirty, or when they move away from home, get married, and have a baby, all that advice begins to take on a new meaning. All the dichos and wisdom that I learned from my family meant a lot more when I had experiences to attach to them.

"Hay que sembrar para recoger"
(You have to sow to reap)

Possibly the most defining part of being a parent is the selflessness that comes from having a child. My advice to all parents is to always think of your children and not yourself. *"Hay que sembrar para recoger"* (You have to sow to reap). If you don't plant good things in your children, you will never sow any fruit.

Part of being a good parent is supporting your child's dreams and goals with strict supervision and selfless support. Teach your children to celebrate their uniqueness. Recognize that your children have special qualities that nobody else in the world has, and encourage them to use those skills and talents to the best of their ability. Here's something else that's not said nearly enough to this generation—don't be afraid of competition! Encourage your children to embrace competition as a way of bettering themselves, rather than as a way of cutting down others.

An important way of building your children's self-esteem, so they will have the courage to venture out, is to show them love and affection willingly and generously. When you kiss, hug, and say "I love you" to your children in public, you implant a sense of respect and security. *"Se enseña con cariño y no con violencia"* (Teach with affection and love, not with violence).

> *"Los hijos son la prolongación de nuestra existencia"*
> (Our children are the prolongation of our existence)

This is my father's favorite dicho. It is the most symbolic of his life and his attitude toward raising children. I believe that he was put on this earth to be a doctor, husband, and an absolutely outstanding father. For my father, setting a good example for his kids has been his life's mission. He incorporates my sister, my brother, and me in everything he does. It's so important to him that his children learn from his sacrifice, determination, and drive, during both good and bad times. The way my father sees it is: Our children are the prolongation of our existence, so I want my existence to be a good one!

Every time I go out in public with my daughter people look at her and say that she looks exactly like me and my mother. It's amazing how strong blood is. The family unit truly is like a child's blood bank from which strength can be gathered for a lifetime.

Teach your children to understand how valuable each and every family member is. Family creates a "value added identity" that infuses a child with a foundation of self-confidence unavailable in the best self-help books. For example, imagine a teenager, uncertain about his future and having no faith that he has any special talents to do anything. Then, during a family reunion he learns that his grandmother was a world-class concert pianist, his grandfather was a math whiz, and his uncle was a talented writer. Suddenly this young man sees new possibilities. It is just as important for parents to convey this valuable information to their children as it is for children to seek out and embrace it.

What kinds of values, morals, and personality traits will you pass on to your children? I hope to pass on to my daughter the same values and lessons that my parents taught me, in addition to those I've learned in my life. I especially hope that she learns to be a compassionate, independent human being, and tolerant of others. I will teach her to be proud of her culture and use it as much as she can.

As a Latina woman, I'll let her know that she is just like everybody else, except she has a special gift. I hope she sees, by observing my life, how amazing it is to be a woman who can be completely committed to her family, her profession, and her community all at the same time. I'll teach her that it's okay to be a workaholic as long as she understands her other roles in life. She has to understand that she is always going to have a role to accept. This is a privilege, not a defeat, just as life itself and all the roles in it are a privilege and not a chore.

Kids (and often parents) are sometimes under the mistaken impression that age eighteen is a cutoff of sorts, just because most young people head off to college or enter the real world then. They like to think they're fully grown and are offended if their parents still refer to them as "my child."

In my family, turning eighteen wasn't some magical age of transition. It didn't mean that we were suddenly adults or that it was time to move out of the house. I was still living with my parents when I got married at age twenty-seven. This is perfectly normal in the Latino community. I clearly didn't feel that I had to grow up at eighteen. I still had the right to be the child of my parents, and my parents expected me to be a child so they could be there to guide me. They still do. It's a mistake for parents to think that just because their child is eighteen, it's time for them to be out on their own, with no further guidance.

You never get away from being your parents' child! In fact, whether you know it or not, as soon as you leave home for the first time (for college or otherwise) you end up trying to emulate your parents. C'mon, admit it! The way you interact with others, cook, clean, and look after yourself—who does this remind you of? You are an exact reflection of the people you have been trying to separate yourself from for a lifetime. As much as you try to be independent, what you are subconsciously doing is becoming your parents.

For example, when I moved out on my own I remember trying to season my cooking the same way my mother does.

And it didn't stop there. I found myself trying to resolve problems, maintain harmony, clean the house, and take care of my friends—exactly the way I learned from my mother. During a trip to Spain in law school with my friends, they had the time of their lives—while I worried where everyone was, what they were doing, and if they had eaten enough. As they partied every night, I waited back at home like a worried mother. I was so overly dramatic! I still laugh about this story thinking about it to this day. I was being their mother because that's what I knew how to be.

Many children are raised without the presence of one or both parents, typically because both need to work. But it is the hand of the parent, the guidance given to the children, morally and spiritually, that lasts a lifetime. I have found that it is not the amount of time but the quality of time spent between parent and child that matters. My father was away from our family for long periods while studying in medical school and working; however, it was the quality of time that he spent with me that shaped our relationship then and now. One of the strongest relationships I have today is with my father. He is also my mentor and confidant on marital and career issues.

Remember, that just as you were influenced by your parents, your children's foundation will be shaped by you. How we speak to them, how we love them, how we listen to them, and how we look them in the eyes has an irreversible and permanent effect on them. Our children become a reflection of ourselves.

"La ropa sucia se lava en casa"
(Wash your dirty laundry at home)

Never argue in front of other people or your kids. I'll admit that Christopher and I need to work on this one! When you argue in front of others or bring your arguments outside of your home into theirs by recounting or gossiping about your partner, it brings negative attention to your marriage. This means never talking negatively, even to your parents, about your spouse because it taints how they view them. They get a one-sided view that is not fair to your partner. And when you argue in front of your children, be aware that they are young and are not able to distinguish between "good fighting" and "bad fighting" and the experience can be very scary for them. Keep your arguments behind closed doors.

QUICK TIP

Make time for your children:
Read to your child. Parents can add to the journey of education and life by choosing books with characters and stories that shape their kids' minds and morals.

CHAPTER EIGHT

Setting a Positive Example

"La familia es lo único que tenemos con toda certeza"
(With all certainty, family is the only thing we have)

This is not a dicho but a valuable lesson I learned from my mother. Family is the thread that unites spouses, parents, and children. Family is what unites all human beings. In time of tragedy, it is often our family that helps us to overcome. In times of joy, it is often our family that helps us to celebrate. And even though we may have conflict and problems with some of our family members, it's been my experience that our families will never fail us when we really need them.

One of the most heartfelt lessons I will teach to my daughter, and I hope all parents will teach to their children, is the importance of staying close to one's family. Closeness does not necessarily have to be geographical. Although this does remind me of how just a short time ago, many generations of one family would live, love, and die under one roof. When family members became ill, the family rallied to care for them. There was no nursing home to conveniently ship a person to, or hospice care to come in and take over the family's duties. The family did it because that's what family is for. These days, some believe it is a burden and even an injustice to have to care for a sick family member. People often lament, "I *have* to see my family for the holidays! How ever will I survive the three-day ordeal?" Sometimes I wonder if they're referring to their family or their arch rivals!

A single mom and her sixteen-year-old daughter came into my TV courtroom to settle a monetary dispute. The daughter had gotten pregnant by her over-age boyfriend and decided to have an abortion, but did not have the money. Mom agreed to pay for the abortion, on the basis that the daughter and boyfriend would pay her back—apparently this was her way of teaching responsibility. It's not a dicho, but the phrase "the horse is already out of the barn" is what springs to mind. Her daughter paid her back but the boyfriend did not, and now the mom was suing the boyfriend for the abortion money. How did the lines of intention and action become so tangled in this family? They had such a misconception of what family is and how they should be sticking together instead of running away from each other. You teach your children by example.

I didn't blame or judge the mother. Instead, my heart went out to her. She was obviously doing what she thought was best for her child. At the same time, as the parent she has to teach her daughter to take responsibility for her actions. This particular mother was just going about it the wrong way. She should have had a conversation about responsibility with her daughter before she got pregnant. Now it was too late. Instead, this mother let her friend role get in the way of her parent role and the responsibility lesson was lost.

I looked at the mother and said, "I know you think you're doing the right thing, but you need to focus on your daughter. She needs a mother, not a friend. Be there for her." Then I looked at the girl and told her, "You need to know that your boyfriend is destroying your family and your life. If you don't put him aside you won't have anybody. You need your family." Her boyfriend was disrespectful and condescending and though her mother had tried to warn her, the daughter had blown her off. The most heartbreaking moment was seeing how destroyed this girl was, because there in my courtroom, she finally understood that this boyfriend was nothing but trouble. She finally understood that what had happened to her possibly could have been prevented with a little guidance and wisdom from Mom.

Sometimes parents don't realize the narrow window of time and opportunity in which they have to teach their children the most valuable lessons in life. So often, parents say, "I'll teach her that someday" and "When the time is right." And then someday comes, the lessons were never taught, and it's too late. The dichos, values, and wisdom passed on to me from my family that I am now passing along to you and hopefully your children, are meant to be learned, and lived by today. Talk to your children right now about the values you hold closest to your heart—don't wait.

Why is the importance of family not emphasized enough? Have you ever noticed how the people you surround yourself with tend to have backgrounds similar to yours? This is not an accident. They probably learned the same lessons as you and had the same type of role models. In the case of the single mom and her pregnant daughter, those lessons and role models were shaky at best, or the girl would not have been drawn to this irresponsible boyfriend. The people around you probably play by the same rulebook as your family. A good family foundation transcends any cultural difference. You can instantly be friends with someone if they have the same family values you do.

Yet the perception of family has somehow transitioned from support to baggage. Historically speaking, everything else around us in society, from sociopolitical trends, crime, morality issues, and education seems to stem from the consensual perception of family. When the majority of people convey a casual attitude about family, especially in front of their children, they affect society. Family creates society. It is the most defining human characteristic and value we have as a group. By raising Sofia, I'm creating a new member of society. It is so important to instill the love and respect of family in our children. This attitude will allow them to deeply respect other parts of their life. Without respect for family, they will never respect themselves, others, or life as well. They will find it easy to be rude and demeaning to others. Those are casual behaviors—sarcasm is very easy to slide into with barely any effort if there isn't a compass intact to prevent it.

One of my greatest experiences while shooting my show *La Corte de Familia* was dealing with issues that affect the family. Those experiences reinforced my belief that issues of family, love, and trust are more important than money.

Family acts as our moral and ethical compass. We need to wake up and be aware of the messages we communicate to our children by our actions or lack thereof. As a society how are we going to achieve great things with a casual attitude? If nothing really matters and everything is disposable, from income to marriage, then what is worth creating?

I hope and pray that Sofia never refers to Christopher and me as "those people I have to see twice a year for holidays," but I doubt that she would, based on the lessons of family I teach her every day through my words and actions. I am blessed that my parents instilled the value of family in me.

My parents encouraged me constantly. They just knew that I could do whatever I set my mind to. If they could accomplish what they did, I can do more. I open one door and another opens for me. From how they look at me and how they talk to me, their words and actions encourage me, sometimes without their even knowing it.

For instance, when I first landed my new television show, my mother was more excited than I was. After I finished filming the pilot episode and was still worried about how well I did, my mother told me, *"Hay que darle tiempo al tiempo."* (You have to give time time). What she was trying to teach me is that with time everything is always resolved, so why worry about it? She helped me concentrate on other things instead of obsessing about it. The lesson here is to be patient, sometimes one of the greatest challenges in life. My parents provide the constant vigilance and direction I need to focus in life.

"Los niños y los borrachos siempre dicen la verdad"
(Children and drunks always speak the truth)

There was a case on my television show where the two adult litigants were acting like children, while the children stood at their respective sides and looked on in bewilderment. The first neighbor was the single mother of a little boy who liked to play basketball with his friends. The second neighbor was a hard-headed single elderly woman. Somewhere along the line the older woman built a hideous fence between the two houses and the single mother neighbor didn't like it one bit. She called the city about this hideous fence and the city gave the elderly neighbor problems because she constructed the fence without permits. So the older woman of course got mad at the younger woman and the battle was on. Meanwhile, the little boy continued to play basketball with his best friend. The basketballs frequently missed the basket and went over the fence. Only now that there was a battle in progress, the elderly woman chose not to return the basketballs. So Mom got angry and took her elderly neighbor to court to sue her for fifty dollars—the value of the lost basketballs.

Once upon a time, before the reports to the city, unrecoverable basketballs tossed across the fence, and other demonstrations of pettiness, the two adults were actually friends. By the time they arrived in my courtroom, the neighbors had engaged in a full-on feud. I told them both how ridiculous this was and urged them to get over it and become friends again. However, in the end, it was the two kids who remedied the situation and mended the broken fences between the adults. They made the adults shake hands and "be nice" to each other again.

Sometimes the examples that adults set are not always the best for their children to follow. The simplicity of a child's mind can solve most problems. Children are untainted and pure before society ruins them with fear, stereotypes, and misinformation. We need to also learn from children because they can teach us so much. Next time you face a problem, try and see it through your child's eyes. Think of the simple things your parents taught you (or should have): don't lie, don't steal, be honest, be polite, be considerate of others, work hard, and treat everyone the way you would want to be treated.

QUICK TIP

It is inevitable that your children will see you and your spouse occasionally fight, but remember that showing affection with your spouse will have a more lasting effect. Prove to them that a loving relationship can withstand anything.

CHAPTER NINE

Carrying on Culture

"El que no sabe de abuelo, no sabe lo bueno"
(The one who doesn't know of his
grandfather doesn't know what is good)

What does our culture mean to my family? I asked my mother this, and she said that Latino culture is very important because it has given us a piece of our forefathers and has established the importance of family as a base. It has taught us love of God, respect, love of others, and love of our family. She told me how the foundation of our culture has given us proper grounding. Culture teaches us to take care of and protect each other, our elders, our grandparents, our spouses, and our children. The Latino culture makes sure that we are responsible from generation to generation and that we firmly continue this legacy.

My parents have never been embarrassed by our Latino culture, nor have they ever tried to hide it. In fact, though my mother has been a U.S. citizen for over thirty years, she still has a heavy accent, and is proud of it. My mother and father incorporate "the Pérez" into every aspect of their life—their personalities, cultural identities, language, social interactions, business, and in everything they do, every day. Through their words and actions, my parents have taught me the importance of using the roots of a family tree to carry on our Latino culture with strength and conviction.

I can only hope to have inherited the charisma that comes from being Latino. Those who know my father speak so highly of him because he truly is *the* dynamic Latino man. He has the dazzling smile, presence, handsome looks, and inner security. You can see in his eyes the love and admiration he has for others. He is not afraid to use everything his parents taught him, including the Latino culture, when associating with someone. That, for me, is beautiful. My mother is an equally dynamic, unique, well-rounded little Latina! Everywhere she goes, people marvel, "Oh that Aracelly!" She treats people with warmth and sincerity, wrapped in a completely no-nonsense, straightforward, blunt way of communicating. Culture is who you are, so why bother hiding it?

At home, my mother made sure the refrigerator was never empty, there was always fresh fruit in abundance, and the house was clean and ready to welcome visitors. This is very characteristic of most Latino women. The idea is to make what you have stand out and be welcoming to others. Sometimes Christopher will ask me, "Why are you fixing up the house? Why are you buying flowers? Nobody else is here." I tell him, "We're here."

My parents have preserved the Latino culture in our family by following the examples of their parents and everything they taught them. My grandparents' teachings, faith, dedication, sacrifices, and beliefs have given our family the benefit of an unbreakable moral base. Combining that with the modern-day teachings and ways of doing things has made us all responsible for continuing this legacy. Really knowing your *abuelo* (grandfather), as the dicho says, adds immeasurable value to your family's legacy.

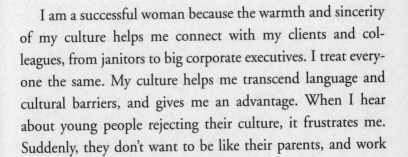

"Nadie está contento con lo que tiene"
(Nobody is happy with what they have)

I am a successful woman because the warmth and sincerity of my culture helps me connect with my clients and colleagues, from janitors to big corporate executives. I treat everyone the same. My culture helps me transcend language and cultural barriers, and gives me an advantage. When I hear about young people rejecting their culture, it frustrates me. Suddenly, they don't want to be like their parents, and work hard at hiding heavy accents, and refuse to speak Spanish.

I asked my mother why she thinks some of the younger Latinos try to run away from their culture. She brought up the really interesting idea that the American Dream is a double-edged sword. Immigrants come to the United States to fulfill their own idea of the American Dream. In their desire to as-

similate they sometimes forget their own customs and traditions. They are afraid that keeping cultural traditions alive will
conflict with their children's new life and new opportunities in
America. But to maintain our identity we must take a risk, as
expressed in the dicho, *"El que no arriesga, no pasa el moro"*
(The one who doesn't risk won't overcome obstacles). Part of
one's identity is language.

For example, I know many immigrant parents who refuse
to speak to or teach their children their native language. Are
they ashamed or afraid that their children will be discriminated against? It is a vicious cycle that doesn't make any
sense. Parents should stop teaching their children to be
something they're not. One of the most wonderful, inspiring
aspects of the American Dream is that the potential for personal greatness increases every time we add a new culture or
tradition to it.

Why do we feel that somehow we must hide our culture as
minorities? The somewhat pejorative term "minority" is not
reality. The numbers speak for themselves. With that said, it is
ironic that even today I face some of the same obstacles my
parents faced when they arrived in the United States, specifically racism and gender discrimination. I face it as a bilingual
woman and as a Latina. But I also know that these have been
and continue to be key factors in my success. As a lawyer, I remember calling professional baseball players' agents and attor-
neys only to respond to their first question with "No, I am not
the attorney's secretary, I am your clients' attorney."

I never got angry but rather viewed my response as an opportunity to set the record straight. I was not programmed to

believe my gender and ethnicity would ever be a hindrance. In fact, I became more determined to become a better lawyer. I strived to become the best. Why would I hide the fact that I am a bilingual Latina woman? It has been my language that has helped me reach thousands of people and given me a special way to connect with anyone in any walk of life.

I am blessed to have the opportunity to reach out and speak to the public every day through my television shows. I show the world what one Latina is in the face of many misperceptions: an educated, no-nonsense, respectful, and compassionate person.

It is important to learn how to work your culture for your benefit. You can talk to somebody you've never met and have their life story in five minutes. That charisma has made all Latino things hot. Today it appears more acceptable to live within both cultures simultaneously and comfortably. Everything we do as a community is observed, digested, and commented on by the media. The Latino culture is suddenly so popular because we're finally coming out of our shells and people are taking notice.

It's not just Latinos, either. People do not realize the wealth of power they have on their side because of their culture. It is a toolbox we forget we have. Every group has a culture—whether it's ethnic, racial, geographical, or religious. Groups create cultures where there wasn't one before. It is a natural part of life to be connected to something greater than yourself. This is an important lesson to pass on to your children.

Today, ironically, to the chagrin of some politicians, I think society is so much more accepting of immigrants and different cultures in this country. Cultural and familial teaching processes are much easier now with fewer obstacles. For example, today's entertainment geared toward young children celebrates diversity, educates, and promotes tolerance rather than discrimination and ignorance. Parents should take these cues and educate their children about their culture so they know it inside and out. It's important that they know what it's all about and how powerful and important it is.

Christopher and I have spoken to our *"cosa preciosa"* daughter, Sofia Daniella, in Spanish and English since her birth. I speak Spanish to her and Christopher speaks to her in English. We will teach her about my Colombian (and adopted Mexican) traditions and my husband's Puerto Rican traditions.

It is not hard to maintain your beautiful traditions. You can do it through food, holidays, and family gatherings. Traditions are a *great* excuse to get together and eat! Food feeds a culture. In our family, we have some crazy traditions that I love because they bring us closer together. When we celebrate New Year's Eve, one minute before midnight we each have to eat twelve grapes. Don't ask! We also have to wear new red or yellow underwear, burn incense throughout the house, and throw rice in the corners of the house for good luck in the upcoming year. Another of our traditions has us packing a suitcase, putting it in the trunk of the car, and driving around the block and back, for many travels during the year. The idea, once again, is good luck.

Sofia has always been exposed to everything about our culture in a very positive way. She has learned all the "good stuff" about being Latina—the values of being at home with her family and extended family, Latin music, and how to speak Spanish and English. Christopher and I have intentionally exposed Sofia to the world, rather than keeping her confined as many small children unfortunately are. We take her out to restaurants and diverse places, travel with her and expose her to a mix of atmospheres in order to keep her open minded and curious about her different cultures. Much of this comes from my experiences growing up in a variety of living situations, moving from country to country, and experiencing cultural extremes. I'm thankful to my parents for exposing me to such a colorful life, because I can see the positive effects this had on me.

I think that if Sofia can take advantage of the beauty of both her American and Latino culture, she will be more sensitive to others and the world in general. Her Latino culture is part of who she is, it will always be a part of her, and she should be proud of it. My niece Isabella is the perfect example of a proud Latina. She is in the second grade at a posh little prep school. She happily tells people how she's half Mexican and half Colombian, stating her name, accent intact, with pride. Isabella loves to go to Mexico, get her hair braided, and come back to school to show it off. She loves how she is the teacher's pet in Spanish class. Isabella's father makes it fun to learn the traditions of the Mexican culture. For example, on the *Día de los Muertos* (Day of the Dead) they set up a makeshift shrine with pictures of family members who have recently passed away to celebrate their lives, and then they go to East Los Angeles to get tamales. My sister and brother-in-law instill culture in such a way that Isabella is attracted to it.

If I can teach Sofia to be just as proud of her traditions, she will have a lot of power in her life. Connecting in different ways with others will open new doors for her and give her a sense of security that nobody can take away. I often marvel that even though she's only a toddler, she already has so much history behind her! If parents and their children learn to recognize this, it will empower them too.

Overall, I think Sofia is going to have an easier time of being multicultural, being a Latina. I think that society is beginning to respect diversity. They're starting to understand that America is a melting pot and the opportunity to welcome new cultures is beneficial to everyone. Twenty years from now Sofia is going to have a great time, because things will only progress. I don't think she's going to run into the same barriers that minorities have previously faced. Women's suffrage, civil rights movements, and the steps that today's Latinos are taking to promote knowledge, understanding, and acceptance of current and future multicultural generations of people have done so much to move society forward and create more opportunities than ever.

As this is all happening, my advice to Sofia will be to always remember what her mother and grandmother taught her: Stay close to your values and traditions and everything will be okay. She has to understand that there will always be some degree of racism and sexism, but I do think she's going to have a better time of it than the generations of remarkable relatives that preceded her, paving the way for her future.

My grandparents lived in their native Colombia in South America, and therefore didn't necessarily have any cultural challenges to overcome, in the sense of immigrating to a new country. My parents were the first in their family to immigrate to the United States and experience the typical culture shock that occurs when immigrants arrive in a completely foreign land and must learn to survive. It was such a challenge for them to get work, despite their education or experience. They were not able to work at their level because they were in a completely new culture. You can see how being an immigrant is a huge blow to your self-esteem and self-worth.

Due to language, educational, professional, and cultural barriers, new immigrants suddenly find themselves at the bottom of the totem pole. I know a woman who was a very successful psychiatrist in Peru and now, because of the cultural barrier of immigrating to the United States, is a nanny. People don't understand that just because someone is an unskilled worker here doesn't mean that that's all they are and all they ever were. My parents, even after being here for forty years, still find themselves facing these assumptions.

On some level, barriers are created by ignorance. Sometimes people just forget to think and consider what they're saying before the words leave their mouth. If they would just stop and think about the implications of their words and the effect they will have on others we could make significant strides toward solving this kind of naivete.

The most difficult multicultural challenge I've had in my life is being part of both worlds—born in the United States, raised in Mexico, and then raised here as a Latino American citizen. Latino is who I am, it is my first culture, and Spanish will always be my first language. Balancing these worlds has been my greatest challenge. I had to find a way to use both of them to my benefit. I am not held back just because I'm not one hundred percent of either world. I've realized that being of both worlds is more of a special gift than anything else. I have integrated all the opportunities given to me by respecting my origins and immersing myself in my traditions. I have done this without shortchanging one world or the other, not being one hundred percent of either, and always being proud of both.

As for Sofia, I hope she won't have these cultural challenges, because she will have learned the happy medium of balancing and incorporating both of her cultures without sacrificing the best of either. Her ancestors, in a way, paid her cultural dues. This is something for parents to consider. After all, wouldn't you do anything for your child? Immigrants ultimately do this for their children. They take the racism, discrimination, and hatred all for the benefit of their children.

Teach your children not to forget where they came from. On my television show, when people were rude to each other, cheated, or created a bad relationship for themselves, I would ask, "Is that how you were raised? Is this what you learned from your family? What went wrong in your life that you went in such a different direction from how your parents raised you?" *"Debes estructurar tu vida de una manera que te acuerdes siempre de quien eres"* (Structure your life in a way so that you will always remember who you are). I hope Sofia can create a life that always reminds her of who she really is and the value of her traditions. And remember, *"Las palabras mueven, pero el ejemplo arrastra"* (Words can move you, but examples are everlasting).

QUICK TIP

Expose your child to the flavors of your culture. Whether through food or salsa dancing, cultural activities are a delightful way to pass on beloved traditions.

Lessons for the Workplace

CHAPTER TEN

Confused Feminism

*"¿Usted no sabe que de la mujer nace el hombre? Somos
indispensables"*
(Do you not know that of the woman the man is born? We
are indispensable)

I believe the entire feminist movement was started simply after too many men insulted too many women with those infamous words: "You're just a woman. You don't know anything." Women finally said "enough is enough" and created feminism to shut the men up! Okay, maybe that's not the official historical version, but it is certainly valid to say that out of women men are born. Without women there would be no men, so they should be careful of how they treat us.

In the Latino culture, women were historically considered

weakest but still the most important part of the family. My father firmly believes that the reason women were traditionally kept at home, worshipped, and overprotected, is because they were the foundation of the family. In those days of the past, work outside the home was not even an option for women. They had to be at home protecting and serving their family. Does this sound like "the weaker sex" to you? Sometimes a man's conception of weakness is backward. With all of the roles and responsibilities that they have to juggle, women have never been weak. They haven't been given the opportunity for weakness!

My father, on the other hand, has always acknowledged that the role of a woman, especially the "housemother," is the hardest job in the world. He jokingly refers to mothers as "slaves." Now combine that with a "working woman" and you have an extremely valuable human being. If aliens looked down and observed various women's roles, especially the power women have at home and in the office, wouldn't they naturally assume that women were the most powerful beings on our planet? It certainly would appear that way, yet the "you're just a woman" syndrome still lingers.

On my television show, male litigants frequently complained, "My wife only takes care of the kids and the house!" as if her job were easier than his. So many times, I wished I could have ordered the man to stay home and do his wife's job for two weeks and then report back to me. It would have been fun to watch as the man came skulking back into my courtroom saying, "It was hell! I hated it! My poor wife!" As the expression goes, don't judge until you walk a mile in another man's shoes, or in this case, gentlemen, your wife's slippers and slingbacks.

So, after extolling the virtues of traditional wifely values throughout the book, it must be obvious that I am really not a feminist, right? I am a 1950s sitcom wife, through and through! Wrong. The truth is I am both things—traditional homemaker and empowered professional. I think I just heard Gloria Steinem's head explode somewhere.

When I first learned this about myself, around 2003, I started calling myself a "confused feminist": *(n)* One who wants it all in the workplace and also wants it all at home. At that time, I had so much on my plate: a successful law practice and television and radio shows, and on top of all that I was pregnant. Yet I would still rush home from taping the TV show and ask my husband, "Are you okay, babe? Did you have a good day? What can I make you for dinner?" I worked at this rate until I gave birth to Sofia. I soon got tired of myself—wanting to be treated like a woman but also wanting to prove that I wasn't weak, just because I was pregnant.

Even beyond the pregnancy I felt I had much to prove—that I was independent, smart, but still a woman at the same time. Both weak and strong together, being a woman but not being treated like a woman. See how much I thought I had something to prove but I really had nothing to prove? In reality, most people see me as a lawyer first anyway. It's all in our heads that as women we have to communicate a grandiose message of our identity to the rest of the world—as if they really care. We need to relax and become normal human beings without trying so hard to prove ourselves.

Sound familiar, ladies? I know I'm not the only confused feminist out there, so stand up and be counted! Being a confused feminist means that it's sometimes easy to forget you're a woman in the purest sense of the word. Our battle cry is along the lines of: Don't mess with me at work but take care of me at home. Wanting my husband to bring home all the bacon wouldn't make me any less of a feminist.

I have a group of close male friends whom I attend law conferences with. They take good care of me: opening doors for me, not letting me pay for anything, ensuring my safety wherever we go. My husband loves that I have such thoughtful friends and takes comfort in knowing that someone is taking care of me when he's not there to do it. A feminist might feel as if those gentlemanly actions somehow diminished her strength as a professional woman, and tell them "I can take care of myself!" It's such a lovely contradiction how these men, my equals, treat me like their daughter or sister. I can turn around just as easily and kiss and hug them, straighten their ties, and match their clothes. They don't think of me as a silly woman or as someone trying to prove something to get something in return. I'm just being myself, as a genuine friend, and a genuine woman. They're not confused, so why should I be?

The other person who is not confused about the many hats I wear is my husband. There is nothing equal about a marriage. However, it has helped that my husband and I have a balanced relationship because we depend on each other and know our roles. This has helped us develop a level of respect, admiration, and healthy dependence on each other. If others adopted this attitude, they would have stronger relationships. What results is a feeling of comfort and confidence from truly having a union, a marriage that gives both partners solace. My husband and I understand each other as human beings and know what values are important to the other. Granted, we're both human and argue, but the foundation of balance is always there.

In any marriage we expect so much from the other person without explaining why we expect it. Women are exceptionally good at criticizing their husbands! At the end of the day my husband respects me as a good business person, a wife, and a mother. He appreciates me and is attracted to me more for being a balance of those roles. It says a lot about Christopher that he is not threatened by me. It also says a lot about the comfort level in our relationship—the emotional intimacy so vital to maintaining a marriage. Acknowledging all of your roles builds self-esteem, and there is nothing confusing about that.

"Querer es poder"
(If you want it, you can do it)

My husband tells me all the time, "You have what you say. You say what you have." If you really want something you can do what it takes to achieve it. You just have to believe in it. Young or old, man or woman—if you want something badly enough and put your mind to obtaining it, you will eventually have it. This is a powerful dicho that crosses gender lines.

I was introduced to feminism when I was in school and read about Elizabeth Blackwell (1821–1910), the first female doctor in the United States. I learned how she was discriminated against and chastised just for being a woman throughout her admissions process and through most of her medical school experience—until she graduated first in her class. I said to myself, "Whoa! People didn't like her because she was female and a doctor." Even as a child that was offensive to me. At that moment I realized, just from reading her story, that women have a harder time than men simply because we're female. Surprisingly, knowing that didn't bother me. I understood that I was not going to change society. This incredible woman gave me a profound awareness and I've never forgotten her. From Elizabeth Blackwell, I learned the concept of feminism before I learned the word. However, as great as the experience was, I can't tell you truthfully that she lit a fire in me.

I draw my strength as a woman from my family. Does that really surprise you? The reason for this strength is my father, the "head" male in our family, the traditional Latino man . . . and the complete contradiction. My father raised me, my sister, and my brother with the same "go get 'em" attitude. He told us all that we could do whatever we wanted, never differentiating between me and my brother. Being female never came up except for early curfews, or ordering my brother, José, to go to parties with me, which was just a father taking care of his daughter, not chauvinism.

My father's advice to all of us was "make sure you finish school, be happy, and choose what you want to do." By treating and empowering us equally, my father taught me indirectly what feminism is. It was very unusual for such a traditional Latino man to do that, so now I appreciate it even more. He is quite possibly the root of my confused feminism. Was my father the *real* first confused feminist?

Feminism is similar in Latino and American cultures. What may be called an overpowering woman in America is a *vieja* in Latino-American culture. Both refer to the women who men in both cultures feel are nagging annoyances and ogres, particularly in the workplace. My male friends often tell me, "You're not a typical *vieja!*" They are referring to women who feel they have something to prove and aren't afraid to let it be known to everyone around them, all the time. Those women say, "You must respect me because I'm a woman!" I say, "You respect me because I'm a good human being, a professional just as smart as you are if not smarter, and I just *happen* to be a woman." Gender in my head has always been secondary, because that's how my father always described it to me. When men see this approach, they treat you like a professional *and* a lady.

My mother also told me over and over, "Mija, you can do whatever you want." However, unlike my father she brought up gender, saying, "You're a woman but you can do whatever you want." I respect this because it was my mother who always wanted to be a lawyer but could not because she was the oldest female, the matriarch of a very big family. She is smarter, more lively, creative, well balanced, and more resourceful than any person I know. So when she brings up gender I know it is a positive thing. When I told my mother

my first dream of being a doctor, she said, "You can do it because there are women who are doctors." Thank you, Dr.
Blackwell.

"Chiquita, pero cumplidora"
(Tiny but reliable)

⤬

Today's Latina is part of the fastest-growing ethnic group
in the country. We are complex, and long to be understood.
Regardless of education, Latinas believe we can have it all—be
a good wife and mother and have a career at the same time.
The secret, or at least my secret, in making it in mainstream
America, while still holding on to my roots and culture, is to
listen and follow the wisdom passed down from my Latina
predecessors through dichos.

The message here is clear: "Size doesn't matter!" As the
daughter of a tiny powerhouse, take it from me, the size of a
person isn't necessarily related to talents and accomplishments. Though my mother is petite in size, her lessons remain profound. She taught me that class could not be
bought; humility was not something one could learn; kind-
ness and compassion took less energy than any other emotion; a lady should always be a lady; and beauty is a reflection
of your deeds. She also taught me not to do anything for personal gain, because nothing would come of it; do things
because you believe in them.

Women like my mother are typical Latinas. Is this why
today's Latinas can wear many hats? Is this why we are so

driven and often feel unstoppable? Is this why we are natural leaders? Is this why we can feed a child, make dinner, talk to our husbands about their day, and fit in a quick call from a client at the same time? Are we trying to compensate for our mothers' lost dreams or are we just riding the wave knowing that anything is possible and that we come from a line of women whose specialty is to multitask and never look back? I feel it is the latter.

We assume a leadership role that is dedicated to serving others, whether it is to our family or our community. In turn, we are the window through which the rest of the world views us. While we may not realize it, all Latinas are critical role models, and our roles carry weight, significant weight, in our personal lives, our community, and the world.

My mother told me that as a woman, I would be responsible for the majority of the work at home. Historically, mothers are workhorses. They must be available twenty-four hours a day, seven days a week. Motherhood is a job with little pay and little respect at times. But it is necessary to bind a community, to bind the family. So, if you are a 24/7 mother and spouse and someone asks you, "Do you work?" your answer should be "Absolutely! I have the most important job with the best rewards, my family and my children and their future."

So, yes, I am tired when I get home from work and yes, I get tired of juggling, but this is my role and I willingly accept it. I am proud to be a devoted and supportive wife and mother. I am proud that for me, both my husband and daughter come first. Family is my greatest strength in life.

"Con la vara que mides, serás medido"
(The standard you judge others
by is how you will be judged)

My parents' encouragement and positive messages really came in handy in one of my first real world experiences—law school.

Law school is difficult; it is emotionally and physically draining. It demands so much from you. I was accepted to law school under a special program called Summer Performance. My grades in college were good, but my Law School Aptitude Test (LSAT) score was not. This program was designed to give applicants such as myself the opportunity to bridge the disparity between university grades, accomplishments, and a standardized test score. We were given the summer to prove that we had what it takes to make it in law school.

Let me tell you, it was challenging. After the first set of exams, my grades were borderline. This frustrated me to no end, because I knew my stuff inside and out. It just did not come out this way on paper. I was crushed. So I made an appointment to see the dean of students for some advice. Well, there I was in front of her, pouring out my heart and asking for help and direction. After she listened and took it all in, and without opening my file or asking me a single question, she simply stated, "Well, maybe law school is just not for you. Maybe you should think of some other career, or maybe just concentrate on raising a family." What??? You can imagine my face, a reflection of how my heart and my soul felt. This was a woman who was supposed to help me. It seemed like this was one woman telling another woman she does not have what it takes to make it in a man's world. I wonder how she felt when I delivered the closing speech at my law school graduation ceremony as student body president.

In the Latino culture the woman is more than the mother—she absolutely is the matriarch of the family. She is saddled with the responsibility of raising kids and disciplining them the majority of the time. Dad is only needed once in a while, so it's easier for Mom to naturally fall into the role of the feared matriarch. Therefore, in the Latino culture mothers are revered and feared. You don't even look at your mother the wrong way, for fear of getting the dreaded "evil eye" in return.

I believe that the concept of feminism is stronger in American culture than in Latino culture. In America, women are more often taught that they should do this, that, and everything else or they're somehow a failure. Who do we think we are in danger of disappointing? If it's our parents, then perhaps the wrong message is being disseminated to young girls. If we as women—Latino or otherwise—did not feel that we have to constantly prove ourselves so much, then maybe the other challenges in our life (children, spouse, personal life, stress, health, work, etc.) might just work themselves out.

I believe that in today's culture women can have a voice and a business, can run a boardroom—and in the middle of that boardroom your nanny can call, telling you that your baby has a fever, and nobody will blink an eyelash. Feminism is more than how Gloria Steinem imagined it could be in the 1970s. Being female today is being able to be a woman in every aspect while having an equal role in business, politics, and the community. Men are also being helped by recent changes. For example, they are given paternity leave after their babies are born. In the past, the woman was seen as the sole caregiver and now men share that role.

In reality, there is nothing confusing about a woman's role. Doors are so much more open because people's heads are finally in the right place. Barriers aren't there anymore unless people choose to put them up. The modern woman of the 1970s struggled to be accepted as a mother, pacesetter, and CEO. Sure, women don't have it easy and we need to prove ourselves more than men. But since that time our role has evolved and society appreciates that. Those who fail to realize this are backtracking themselves.

How can the next generation of women become empowered by these basic principles? Take what your mamí taught you, especially your feminine wiles and charms, and combine them with your common sense and intelligence. While we're not always equal to men in certain aspects such as physical power, knowing our other strengths can take us a long way.

As women, it's okay to be both traditional and empowered at the same time. We can't forget that we're women—daintier and more sensitive than men. We need to be looked after in different ways than men do. There is a high level of sexual and physical violence against women because we are (most of the time) physically weaker and smaller than men. We can't deny that. Some women may say, "Screw you—don't walk me to my car!" But I consider myself a smart woman and you should, too. I could be the CEO of a large corporation and I would still have a man walk me to my car. A six-foot-tall man won't attack a six-foot-tall man. Not wanting to ask for help or protection is what makes you weak.

Women, particularly immigrant women, are the fastest-growing demographic of entrepreneurs in the United States today. According to the November 2005 issue of *Newsweek* magazine, "The percentage of self-employed immigrant women is higher than the corresponding number of self-employed native-born women, and they're even closing the gap with immigrant men . . . [I]mmigrant women can earn extra money without struggling in a hostile workplace or worrying about child care . . . [I]t's also the sign of a changing world. More female immigrants have better education and skills than before, and it is increasingly acceptable for them to work outside the home."

Ironically enough, the majority of their businesses are homemaker and service oriented—such as cooking and house cleaning. What I jokingly call a "confused feminist" is really a woman who understands that the very natural part of being a woman, the traditional caretaking and nurturing feminine being, perfectly complements the professional part, the career-driven, ambitious leader. But regardless of whether a woman owns a cleaning service or a law firm, it is truly good news that we don't have to worry about future generations of young women having to choose between traditional and business roles. Our predecessors have paved a road for women to have the best of both worlds. We should never forget that their struggles directly benefit our futures.

CHAPTER ELEVEN

Values at Work

"El que mucho abarca, poco aprieta"
(One who does too much, does little)

Remember how I said that men have a "sadist" gene while women have a "masochist" gene? This applies not only to marriage but also to work habits. My husband plays golf almost every Friday without the slightest qualm. I, on the other hand, launch into a magnificent guilt complex over a one-hour nail appointment. Why is this? Is it purely biological? I believe it is our natural feminine guilt kicking in. We would much rather serve our business, our clients, and our family than ourselves.

Women historically have been multitaskers. It has been

the role of the woman to have the children, raise and care for them, cook, clean, and serve her husband when he gets home from work. A woman is on call twenty-four hours a day, seven days a week, expected to always comply with her duties rain or shine, in sickness or health. We were raised knowing we would have to raise the kids, cook, and clean simultaneously—Mrs. Cleaver and Ms. CEO all in one. There is a dicho that says, *"La necesidad es la madre del ingenio"* (Necessity is the mother of invention). The necessity of balancing many responsibilities somehow allows us to make things work. This genetic programming has apparently carried over into modern times.

Today's career woman has adopted traditional responsibilities and then added an office workload to her plate as well. At work, women seem to care more about every detail, and worry that they're not living up to their own and other people's expectations. If we cannot take care of it all at once, we get stressed out.

These may be broad generalizations, but I find men seem to just go with the flow, handling the most urgent matters as they arise. They have a unique ability to compartmentalize whatever they're working on, so the rest of the world doesn't seem to be crashing down on them, begging for their immediate attention. Maybe that's why sometimes men are more successful than women—they're firm and sure with their communication, so people are less likely to argue with them. Also, men are less likely to let things get to them. This is an admirable trait if you think about it. They don't have time for guilt because they make sure that they tend to the most immediate obligations and responsibilities so they can more easily devote their time and attention to their family and friends.

"Al que madruga, Dios le ayuda"
(God helps those who wake up early)

I have a friend in personnel recruiting who has an interview style that quite often throws applicants for a loop. She has a way of quickly reaching people's genuine core, using thought-provoking questions to keep them on their toes. At the end of her interviews she is usually told by the applicant, sighing in relief that the ordeal has ended, "I have never been asked questions like that before. You really made me think." Well, isn't that the point?

After all, what does a recycled resume, template cover letter, and well-rehearsed "why you need me" speech really tell you about an individual? Anyone can say they're hard workers, able to handle many responsibilities at once. Show me what you are! People are so busy trying to substitute buzz words for actual personality. Be a real person, not a resume.

Women who are successful in business concentrate on delivering the goods and completing the task. These women don't have time to think about the "extras," the "garnish." Real multitasking is about real results. Thinking about my career thus far, I realize that I haven't climbed any kind of "corporate ladder." I found my own job after law school, started my own law firm, and got into television when people saw my potential.

It's awfully hard to accomplish something if you don't know what the end result should be. Anyone who has ever worked in an organization or taken a business course can tell you that goals should be specific, challenging, and measurable. Yet most business advice is the exact opposite. The "experts" continually throw catch phrases. They tell us to climb the ladder, just do it and don't let anything stop you. Please tell me how any of that is a blueprint for your career. The motivational catch phrases and clichés are all well and good but the only way to succeed is by working hard and being true to yourself.

My "corporate ladder" was set by my parents and so were their instructions to me. There was no hype—just solid advice that anyone could follow and succeed with. You may already have the foundation and work ethics from your parents or mentors that you need to succeed. There is no new cliché or earth-shattering advice that is going to accidentally smash the glass ceiling and give you the magic ride up the corporate ladder, gifting you with a free platter of success. With the wisdom of your family or mentors, all the success you will ever need in life will come to you. My advice to Sofia will be to find something she loves to do and make a living of it. All kinds of success will come from this passion.

QUICK TIP

Have a Mission:
Choose a profession because of passion. Passion will mo-
tivate you more than a paycheck. If you love what you
do, put the time and effort into the job *you* have chosen;
then you will be rewarded with whatever prize you seek.

CHAPTER TWELVE

Cultural Identity

"Dios dijo: ayúdate y yo te ayudaré"
(God said, "Help yourself and I will help you")

When you work diligently, you will be rewarded. It is more important than ever to remember this in a world where there are a multitude of excuses to embrace every time things don't work out exactly how we would like them to. Whether the reason is gender, ethnicity, age, or social status, there always seems to be a little something blocking our way. Is that a valid reason to give up and blame the obstacle for our failure? Or might it be more productive to see the obstacle as a stepping stone to greatness and take responsibility for it? As Harry S Truman said and I'm sure my mother and father would agree, "The buck stops here." Being one hundred percent responsible for using the strengths and abilities that God gave you to overcome cultural, career, personal, and family challenges is the best way I can think of to follow the dicho that begins this chapter—especially when it comes to the cultural identity and discrimination challenges that many face today.

The American workplace is a reflection of the nation's cultural diversity. A mix of cultures and ethnic backgrounds striving for individual success under often cramped company roofs means a whole new set of career challenges for Latinos to overcome.

The levels and types of discrimination start at the door with our accents. For instance, if a Latino goes into a job interview as a Harvard graduate with a heavy accent, it is not rare for the accent to take something away from his accomplishments. I wish we could all understand that a heavy accent doesn't mean that a person's brain is not working.

Here is another example of this kind of cultural discrimination. As my mother was leaving my father's office one day, her car was rear-ended, a minor accident by all accounts. When she got on the phone with her insurance company, speaking to them of course with her very thick accent—perfectly understandable to most people—the woman on the line proceeded to give her the third degree. The woman was very demeaning, repeatedly telling my mother, "I don't understand what you're saying to me! Speak English!" I can tell you that if that had been a face-to-face conversation, my mother would have slapped that woman silly. The ridiculous woman put a translator on the phone, which was completely insulting to my mother and unnecessary. When the woman found out through the translator what kind of car my mother was driving, a nice one, mind you, she rudely asked if my mother owned the car. On top of that, the woman asked my mother five times if the accident was her fault. My mother finally said, "No, it wasn't my fault and you should be on my side!"

The media and entertainment industry also seems to misunderstand just how much cultural variety exists in this country. It bugs me when mainstream television needs someone for a Latino role and the character is only supposed to speak Spanish, and they cast an actor or actress whose Spanish is absolutely horrible. Don't tell me that they couldn't go out and find a fantastic actor who spoke Spanish well. Their priority is to get the job done rather than make the effort to represent other cultures respectfully and accurately. Yet the Latino market and consumer potential is enormous. We are finally being represented in the media. Our thick accents are finally being heard.

However, there is still work to do and a continued presence is needed to assist the next generations of young Latinos who are eager to make their marks. We need to let our communities and our nation know who we are and what we stand for. We must take the visions of our past mentors and make them a reality for Latinos everywhere. It's time to attain more respect, and our mentoring relationship with other Latinos is the launching pad to make that happen. The Latino voice is louder than ever and in order to continue our success we need to turn the volume up.

You may ask yourself, are we really so unknown? Well

when I look at a group of photos of all of the United States presidents, I see forty-three white men. How does this group reflect America, the greatest cultural melting pot in the world? It does not reflect my America. How have we come this far and not come far at all? And why is such a big deal made when people try to "break through" the obvious discrimination, as if it's so preposterous an idea for a minority or woman to have power and be treated equally? These are not medieval times and we should know better than that. The biggest deal of all should be made of the people who propagate the insane notion that equality is some abstract theory or notion that would never work in reality. But we can overcome this. Just as the dicho teaches, we only need to help ourselves to be helped.

"Nadie sabe para quién trabaja"
(No one knows who they really work for)

Don't worry about whom you're working for. Be yourself, while educating yourself. Be the best that you can, work as hard as you can, and prove yourself for yourself. I learned from my mother and father that if you don't do that for yourself, if you don't make yourself proud and happy, then you have created the first and last obstacle to your success. I want you to be out there as a success, representing the Latino culture in all its purity, passion, and empowerment—without looking back!

When I started working in immigration law, I found that

being Latino, I tended to attract people from my own cultural base—an instant set of clients. This is true of most Latino professionals. When you go out into the workplace, never forget your cultural identity, because it instantly separates you from others. Why would you hide something that can give you an edge? When you interview for a job, your cultural identity should be the very first thing that you mention, and talk about it with pride. Being Latino only opens doors that you never realized were there. It gives you causes to fight for, fire in your belly, and a sense of community activism. Use the passion and power of speaking your mind and it will only help you advance and succeed in your career.

All the while, remember that as a Latino in the workplace you are setting the standard for future Latino generations. Whatever you do will create opportunities that other Latinos will enjoy in the future. Never forget this responsibility.

QUICK TIP

Love your roots:
Dedicate your time to cultural organizations that promote networking, mentoring, and friendship. Just do a quick online search and you're sure to find one nearby.

Lessons for a Woman's Spirit

CHAPTER THIRTEEN

Battling Each Other

"El ladrón juzga por su condición"
(We judge others as we judge ourselves)

Men and women approach friendship differently. I have been blessed with many friends, both male and female, and it is definitely easier to maintain friendships with men. They are low maintenance—they don't require daily, weekly, or even monthly phone calls. I can call a male friend after a month and it will seem as if we just spoke yesterday.

Women, on the other hand, are high maintenance. We seem to carry around an inordinate amount of self-judgment, guilt, and ridiculously high standards for both our personal and professional lives. We always feel that we need to say something when sometimes nothing needs to be said. Is it that we're afraid to stop talking because we're afraid people will stop listening? *"La mejor palabra es la que no se dice"* (The best word is the one that is not said). It is actually a sign of healthy self-esteem to realize that you do not always need to be the one talking.

If you think more of yourself you will not need this outside validation and will therefore be much easier on yourself and others. We're so hard on ourselves, trying to be everything to everyone except ourselves. If we were perfect for ourselves first, we wouldn't care what others thought. Insecurity translates into hidden agendas and disclaimers that keep us from really letting go and enjoying life. Women famously preach about living in the present, yet we're the worst at it!

When we look at other women, we see ourselves. And when unhealthy energy bubbles up in us, it's very easy to project it onto another woman—when in reality it's our stuff, not theirs, that's bothering us. When you are in constant battle with yourself and someone else enters the battlefield, you will naturally aim and fire. Since men aren't battling themselves and each other, they won't fire back—end of war. Women, on the other hand—well, duck and cover! Women are obviously not afraid of competition—we're just always in competition with ourselves.

The unfortunate result of all this nonsense is that we're often very hard on each other. For example, when I forget to call a girlfriend for a while, I become more and more afraid to call her because it's been so long. I'm afraid of how she might judge me: she may think I'm a bad friend for "ignoring" her for so long. I eventually realize that these are my own insecurities. If I call my friend and start apologizing profusely and telling her how badly I feel, I'm most likely planting thoughts in her head that may not have previously been there. Suddenly, the bond that connects us is muddied with all kinds of negative feelings that do not belong there, and certainly aren't going to create a healthy relationship. *"Es mejor callar que locamente hablar"* (It is better to be quiet than talk crazy).

I think that women sometimes use the word "friend" too loosely, without honoring the meaning of the word. After a woman's first friendship goes badly, the tendency is to always question the integrity of all future relationships with women. When a woman calls you "my friend" you wonder what that means, but we have created this ambiguity for ourselves. Men, on the other hand, would lie on railroad tracks for their friends.

Understand your relationships and understand yourself. Drop the guilt and insecurities and you won't have anything to fight about. If you don't start a cycle of unhealthy energy, chances are your friends won't either. Let's encourage the best in each other, not the worst! As women we need to be less high strung, and take things less personally so that we are open to and accepting of the heartfelt, close relationships with each other that we all deserve. Just remember, as my mother says, *"Amigos, oros y vinos cuando mas viejos mas finos"* (Friends, gold, and wine, the older they are the more valuable they are).

As Elizabeth Blackwell says, what is done or learned by one class of women becomes, by virtue of their common womanhood, the property of all women. If we are insecure, then other women will be insecure around us. For instance, I have noticed that women often do not look each other in the eye when they first meet. Sure, ladies, we've all heard the old joke about which body parts men's eyes are likely to wander to when they first meet a woman. But in reality, men are more likely to look you in the eye and shake your hand confidently. They have nothing to prove, no guard up, and are genuinely pleased to meet you. Women, on the other hand, whether we realize it or not, are more apt to take a step back and look other women up and down before shaking hands. Are these body image issues? Lack of self-esteem? Nine times out of ten, women hesitate, put their guard up, and allow their own insecurities to create a wall of fake niceties between them. We feel that we have to compliment each other, whether the compliment is organic or contrived. All these little nervous "twitches" manage to do is create more space among women. Why do we try so hard to manufacture something artificial when we have the ability and the right to have the same "look you in the eye, get real, and lay everything on the table" connection that men are so good at?

It is a sign of weakness, individually and for womanhood as a whole, when we are petty and insecure. This behavior is extremely obvious to others. It takes away from our intelligence and accomplishments, and minimizes everything else we have worked so hard to create individually, and as a gender. How can we ever expect social or economical equality and respect when we keep taking shots at each other?

As women, our behavior creates a domino effect that can either undermine or uplift our gender. Imagine a woman sure of herself, not trying to be a perfectionist, living day by day in the present and not inflicting "garbage" on herself or other women. Her actions and their positive consequences will create a ripple effect that will become the property of all women, all over the world, for generations to come.

I hope that Sofia learns from my words and example that the most important thing is to treat women and men equally and genuinely. My wish is that she will always befriend and surround herself with confident, secure women and men. I hope she understands that those who don't act that way are insecure, and their actions have nothing to do with her. And above all, I hope Sofia always looks people squarely in the eye when she meets them.

CHAPTER FOURTEEN

Secrets for Staying Young

"Las canas no son vejez, pero el último pelo sí es."
(Gray hair is not a sign of old age, the last hair is)

My mother always taught me that a lady should always be a lady and that beauty is a reflection of self at whatever age. She says it is the beauty that comes from your heart that is displayed physically. *"Hay que envejecer con gracia"* (Grow old with grace). Beauty is not about vanity or looking for outside validation or esteem but is about pride in oneself. She still teaches me by example that it's not about your size; it's not your latest haircut or the types of clothes you wear. Beauty is all about the love you have for yourself. That's what will make people's heads turn.

My mother taught me that beauty is about celebrating

femininity. Part of this is being proud of your physical self. This means looking your best at all times—whether you are at home alone, with your family, or out in public for a fancy night on the town. Why isn't there a difference? Because you're making the effort to look and feel your best for yourself, you're not doing it for appearance's sake. Unfortunately, that kind of natural approach is contradictory to today's concept of beauty.

The idea of "aging gracefully," that our mothers taught us is harder than ever. We now live in a consumer society where Botox, lasers, chemical peels, and advanced cosmetic surgery define beauty and youth and the idea of staying young is completely relative. Beauty and youth are consumer goods, and they accompany wealth and status. Ask any cosmetic or pharmaceutical company—there is money in selling beauty and youth, and they sell well.

I am not sure why we have turned to buying beauty and youth like we buy everything else. Why has our value system changed so drastically that we no longer value the beauty of a laugh line, poignancy of a worry wrinkle, or a natural sag here and there as much as we used to? These days you can walk into a doctor's or dentist's office and pick up a stack of brochures advertising youth or beauty in the guise of health. And as more spas, more cosmetic medical facilities, and more boutique medical offices open up, we turn farther away from the concept of aging. We have become confused and now aging can't take its naturally beautiful course.

Don't get me wrong, I don't think there's anything wrong with plastic surgery or any other type of beauty-enhancing procedures. But only if you're already happy with yourself physically and spiritually and you know that the surgery will complement your happiness, instead of using it to fill an emotional void that surgery or procedure is simply not designed to fill. If looking good outside makes you feel just as good on the inside, I can only applaud you.

I remember when I was a little girl I couldn't wait until I turned thirty. I thought that thirty meant being the perfect adult and the perfect woman. I was in such a hurry to age and become what I thought would be the epitome of beauty. In reality, today in my late thirties, I feel better than I ever did at thirty. I feel more stable, more in tune with myself, my body, and my life. Like a fine wine, I continue to get better with every passing year.

Perceptions of youth change over the years, just as perceptions of beauty have evolved. This may not be remotely detrimental to society, but when the focus is skin deep, what happens to our heart and our spirit?

Where do our values really lie? We constantly have images of youth and beauty pushed at us from the media. And it seems as if we are starting to adopt a perception of beauty and youth that is all about the outside, and nothing about the inside. It is sometimes hard to remember and balance what you have learned from your family about youth and beauty with what is being communicated by the media and society. How do we marry these two contradictory notions?

Did these "media" issues exist when I was growing up? Honestly, I don't remember. Is that because they didn't exist as much as they do today, or because my parents constantly instilled such strong values about aging in me? They didn't make aging a negative issue, so phrases like "pressure to be thin" and the idea of comparing the reflection in the mirror to super-models were not even on my radar. Instead of looking to celebrities, I would look at my mother, then and now. Today at five feet one inch, 150 pounds, my mother may not be what we call a supermodel. But she is such an amazingly put together woman—the Latina Sofia Loren, from her beautiful face and expressive eyes to her elegant hands and dainty fingers—what more could I have asked for in a beauty role model? She was and still is my example of where to look for inner and outer beauty. My mother exemplifies the *refran,* *"Los ojos son el espejo del alma"* (The eyes are the window to the soul). So today I understand the secret to staying young—it starts from your heart.

Youth in Society

"No sólo de pan vive el hombre"
(Man doesn't live on bread alone)
—Matthew 4:4

With a father, brother, and cousin who are all doctors, I have learned that there are no quick fixes for our spirit. They have taught me that many of the so-called minor health problems that people have are simply emotional.

Just as man does not live by bread alone, people cannot live from prescriptions alone. When my father recognizes this after examining a patient, instead of writing a prescription he will insist very strongly that the best remedy for the patient is going for a long walk or engaging in some other type of relaxation that rekindles a sense of youth and revives the spirit. My father has a gift for getting people so excited about this that patients eagerly take his advice, sometimes as soon as they leave his office! So many apparent problems are just about patients needing to feel better about themselves.

My cousin Angie is a physician who has learned that modern medicine benefits from traditional wisdom. She says that keeping people healthy is not just about treating high blood pressure or diabetes or cholesterol. More and more, it is about keeping people whole, and giving them the resources they need to live and thrive in a world that is throwing an awful lot of resistance their way. The world is pushing them to look younger, more beautiful, and stronger. In trying to find a magic solution to offer her patients, she realizes she has what modern medicine cannot offer—she has the wisdom of her family.

More than ever, doctors are called upon to help their patients achieve the balance and peace of mind that is important not only in staying young, but also in warding off many of the things that prematurely age us.

A good first step is to search for wholeness in your approach to life. Realize that health is not just about looking youthful and having good laboratory numbers when you go to the doctor. As my cousin tells many of her patients, there are no life transplants. Wholeness is having a good sense of self and identity, where all parts work together to provide the best quality of life.

"Una buena acción es la mejor oración"
(A good deed is the best prayer)

When my doctor cousin Angie was in Ohio in the third year of her residency, she was approached by a senior social worker who was assisting with the discharge of one of the hospital's few Latino patients. The patient was an elderly woman from Puerto Rico who had been admitted to the hospital for pneumonia.

The patient, let's call her Claudia, had been in Ohio visiting her daughter while on vacation from Puerto Rico. Apparently, two years earlier, Claudia had lived in Ohio independently in a home of her own and had since returned to Puerto Rico. Now, two years later, Claudia was visiting her daughter when she fell ill and could no longer live by herself. The social worker's role was to encourage Claudia to live in a facility that would meet her needs and assist her with daily living. Whether this would be a short-term rehab, assisted living facility, retirement home, or senior residence, the social worker wanted to meet the needs of the patient in the best way possible by using her years of experience and resources. This is what she was paid to do and what she was good at.

During Claudia's discharge from the hospital, it came to the social worker's attention that Claudia fully expected to return and live with her daughter, rather than go to one of these facilities. The social worker approached my cousin, because she was baffled by the idea that Claudia expected the daughter to take her in. The social worker was further confused by the fact that the daughter was willing to take on this responsibility and care for her. The social worker approached Angie because she wanted to understand why the daughter decided to do this.

It's amazing to see how times have changed from when, in earlier times, families all lived together under the same roof. The elderly members were the most revered in the household, and it was a privilege to care for them until they died. I imagine that it was a healthy learning experience for the younger family members to be exposed to the natural processes of disease and dying.

The role of caregiver in the Latino culture is not a role at all. It is the responsibility of the family, and caring for one's family is not considered a chore or an obligation. We embrace this role out of love, respect for our elders, and as a part of our own culture.

My cousin tried to explain this to the social worker. She tried passionately to paint a picture of the fabric of our Latino culture, how tightly woven the generations are, how the elder generations are the most integral part of that woven quilt, and how we foster this caregiver attitude so naturally. In our culture, we cannot function without generations merging together in this fabric. We are cognizant of the fact that our elders are our heritage, our sense of self, our sense of identity, and in a way, a sense of our future.

Now I certainly cannot judge whether this is the perfect situation or not. I also cannot determine whether we as children, offspring, are the best and most adequately equipped caregivers for our parents. Obviously in some cases we are not.

However, I can say with confidence that in the Latino culture, when a family member needs to be cared for we do it willingly. My beloved father-in-law, Ray, who passed away from cancer, spent some of his final days surrounded by family, friends, and of course his beloved Dukes in our home. I cannot imagine this situation playing out any other way. Also, what a blessing it was to spend that time together as a family, sharing in this wonderful man's final days.

Our identity lies in our elders, and they have a great amount of say in the direction of our lives. For us to not have them at our side really would disjoint a pact, deny our heritage, and remove part of our identity.

Celebrating Youth

"Es la ley de la vida"
(It is the law of life)

My father once told me that countless numbers of his elderly patients believe that age truly resides inside one's heart. He observed that when you act young you stay young. My father taught me the difference between "aging" and "becoming old." Unfortunately for all of us, the word "old" has come to mean "useless" in society. A better statement might be that we "mature."

If you start saying and thinking things like "I'm too old," guess what will happen? You stop living. Many people have this attitude that we're supposed to work until age sixty-five and then just wait to die. Or the opposite—people believe that we're supposed to mindlessly and grumpily bide our time working the daily grind and then really start living at sixty-five. But both of these views are wrong. Life starts with every new day.

Your life begins today and you are as young or old as you think you are. Decide to do something different—don't just wait to die. For instance a cancer diagnosis can either be a death sentence—a reason to wait to die—or a reason to renew hope and passion in life, but it shouldn't take a terminal disease to evoke this kind of action. Spend every day celebrating life, no matter what your age, rather than fearing death.

My mother in particular taught me through her actions that we should *"hay que envejecer con gracia"* (Grow old with grace). I hope that Sofia learns the same lessons and gains the same interpretation of youth through my example.

QUICK TIP

Enjoy Chocolate:

Dark chocolate, that is. Scientific studies show that dark chocolate is rich in antioxidants that neutralize free radicals that are believed to contribute to aging. *"Lo que no mata engorda"* (What doesn't kill you fattens you). Everything in moderation.

CHAPTER FIFTEEN

Mentorship

"El diablo sabe más por viejo que por diablo"
(The Devil knows more because he is old, rather than
because he is the Devil)

When my mother tells me this dicho, she is really saying that with age comes experience, and that brings knowledge.

There are no shortcuts in life. But having a tour guide to show you the way certainly can't hurt. It is nice to have someone who can share his or her life experiences with you. A mentor can steer you in both personal and career matters and give you a standard of ethics and values to strive toward on a daily basis. The guidance of a mentor is like the protection a large tree offers on a sunny day: *"El que a buen árbol se arrima buena sombra lo cobija"* (If you find a good tree, its shade will protect you).

The most important mentors and role models, and also the best protectors, that any child could have are their parents. My mother and father were my first mentors, equally and in their own right. It is obvious that my parents were very successful in shaping my life where mentorship was required. With only a few rare exceptions, I think parents should always be a child's most valuable and treasured mentors. There is, however, another category of role models that young people can admire and learn from. I don't want to use the word "celebrity," but every once in a while a well-known or historical figure can greatly inspire a child's personal values or career path.

As I noted earlier, Elizabeth Blackwell, America's first female doctor, empowered me when I was very young. Her story made me feel that my opportunities were limitless. After all, I'm thirty-seven years old and still talking about the woman! This is not to say that she's in the same mentor category as my mother—not even by light years. But Dr. Blackwell did inspire me in a very specific way on my career path.

In some instances, because family is not being reinforced enough or not available, kids are forced to look to outside sources for mentorship—sports figures, actors, and other strangers, but they're not supposed to be your child's primary mentors. Kids need a road map and instruction manual to teach them the most important values in life. The only people who can really teach those values are people who truly care about their well-being and their future.

Parents tell kids the truth and not necessarily what they always want to hear. Sometimes it's easier for kids to get the easy answers from others who don't know or care about them. *"No hay preguntas indiscretas, sino respuestas indiscretas"* (There are no indiscreet questions, only indiscreet answers). This can also be interpreted as "There are no stupid questions, only stupid answers," so children should not be afraid to ask their parents questions.

Parents are in a unique place to constantly inspire their children. But it's important to be aware that there's a big difference between a sound bite like "go for your dreams" and the follow-up actions and guidance that only a parent can provide for a child every single day.

"Dime con quien andas y te diré quién eres"
(Say to me with whom you walk
and I will say to you who you are)

Who you associate with is a reflection of yourself and who you strive to be. Who are the people around you who you want to be like? I look up to people, especially women, who juggle it all—family, a successful business, and giving back to the community. I want to be like every incredible woman who I meet. I specifically admire professional men and women who contribute to the community—ordinary people who contribute their own nonbillable hours in the midst of all of their other responsibilities. These people are part of something greater than themselves. They live outside the board of directors by tutoring, helping kids without parents, and much more.

For me, the most amazing thing is when one of these individuals sits down, looks me in the eye, and shares an insight about why and how they accomplish such wonderful things. With commitment naturally comes challenge—a challenge to make the time and effort for a cause. Some people do it because it's a mandatory part of their job, but I'm more interested in watching people who have a complicated life and family, yet still have enough time to give of themselves. I admire those people who aren't afraid to put their titles and wealth aside just to give back to someone who needs help. Those are the people who really matter.

Humility, sincerity, and sharing are the most important qualities in a mentor. *"Haz bien y no mires a quien"* (Do good and don't expect anything in return). My mentors are men and women who aren't afraid to be themselves and give all they have. Mentors are people who stay true to themselves and aren't afraid to go after what they desire, while always being conscious of others around them. To really go after your goals you have to be somewhat selfish and think of yourself. You can't be afraid to say no once in a while so you can stay focused on your objectives. The most well-rounded people I know are determined, aggressive, ambitious, and know exactly what they want, but never abandon the core of their humanity. Like my father, they are extremely energetic and have never been afraid to overcome obstacles placed in their path. These are the people whom I have always admired and this is how I hope my daughter will be.

I try to be a mentor by example. I will gladly be someone's personal or professional mentor because it's simply a matter of answering: How did you do it? How do you stay true to yourself? How do you maintain a close bond with your parents? How do you stay happy in business? I will embrace the experience as long as the mentor relationship is defined by the sharing of my personal experiences as advice or inspiration for others. I'm not here to create experiences or provide specific guidance for other people's unique lives, and I would hope that all mentors feel that way. I'm not here to tell anyone that they should do something just because it worked for me. I prefer to inspire others the way others inspired me, through example and accomplishments.

I particularly hope that I'm a mentor to Latino kids trying to make it. Again, not by telling them specifically what to do—that's why parents were created. Most important, I want to inspire them to be close to their families because that bond with my family is the real root of everything I have and ever will accomplish.

> *"Los celos se parecen a la pimienta, que si es poca,*
> *da gusto; si es mucha, quema"*
> (Jealousy is like pepper, if you add a little,
> it gives a bit of flavor; if you add too much it burns)

Truly great business and personal mentors are one and the same. They do not hold back but always give one hundred percent of themselves when advising on both personal and business issues. When you take a business mentor out of the corporate world, he is exactly the same as a friend. I've seen it again and again in my own mentors.

One of my business mentors is a very successful woman who built her own law practice and is nationally recognized for her work in her specialty area. After she was married and had a child, she began her own practice to give herself flexibility. With a limited amount of time at her disposal, for the most part she ended up devoting herself solely to her child and her law practice. All of this time and hard work paid off, and she became one of the best in her field. Instead of identifying with this type of drive and ambition, we women tend to be jealous. It's much easier for women to ridicule and try to take away from her success than it is to applaud and emulate it.

This has never made sense to me—women refusing to mentor other women out of jealous paranoia that one will surpass the other. Why is it that the more successful you are, the less women get along with you? A woman mentoring another woman is a completely different dynamic unto itself. In general, women are not as generous to each other as men are. Don't get me wrong, I have met incredible professional women who I was blessed to learn from purely by example. However, in the beginning, getting them to open up and give to me what they freely give to me now was a challenge. I had a tough time because most women just refused to mentor me. Is it a trust issue or a jealousy issue that I do not have more professional women as mentors? Did they fear that I would take their jobs away or be better than they were if they shared even a small fraction of their knowledge with me? Perhaps it was a self-esteem issue—"I don't think I have anything to offer as a worthy mentor so I'll come up with a reason not to do it." The upside of these experiences was that I learned not to be afraid of competition. If you're controlled by competition with others, you will drive yourself crazy. Life is big enough for you and your competition.

Men seem to have mastered the art of mentoring and supporting each other's success while engaging in healthy competition. In the legal business, they refer clients to each other, constantly generating business for one another. Women don't support one another nearly as much. We're all so afraid, constantly wanting to be the best and have a hard time accepting that sometimes we will be and sometimes we won't. Men want to mentor other men to strengthen the team, so to speak. At social professional gatherings, my experience is that men are always more generous with advice than women are. I make it a point to talk to the younger women at the events, because I know how tough it is when you're first starting out and how many millions of questions are swirling around in your head.

If young people seek you out, you've somehow inspired them by saying or doing something that they want to successfully apply to their own life. Trust that you have something of value to share with them. Find the time, put aside your own self-doubt, and if it's a trust or jealousy issue, get over yourself. When someone sees a light in you, the only responsibility you have is to share it with them.

Lessons for
the Immigrant Soul

CHAPTER SIXTEEN

English as a Second Language

"A buen entendedor, pocas palabras bastan"
(For a good listener, only a few words are needed)

One of my first "English lessons" was during the famous "mooo . . ." car ride from Mexico into the United States with my family. I'm sure that I was also exposed to English in Mexico, but until my parents made the choice to move back to America, learning this new language was not a priority for me. Based on my parents' experience as immigrants in this country, they knew that learning English was important. My father encouraged us and told us, "We are in the United States, we all need to learn to speak English." The dicho he used to make this point was *"A la tierra que fueras, haz lo que vieres"* (In the land you go to, do what you see).

He says that you need to respect the customs of the society where you live.

Knowing that I would be going to school with English-speaking classmates also motivated me to master this new language. I remember being really embarrassed because I couldn't communicate with my friends. Just as my mother suffered cultural isolation all the years before in the Bronx and in San Ysidro, I was now suffering language isolation as a child unable to communicate in school.

I felt embarrassed that I spoke Spanish better than English. I'm ashamed to admit that I didn't want to speak Spanish to my mother in front of my friends because I thought they would ridicule me. I think that this is a common sentiment among recent immigrants, especially among children. Here they are in America, speaking English at school and with their friends, and then speaking their native language at home with their family. I felt singled out because I spoke Spanish. It became challenging and uncomfortable because I wanted to be just like my American friends. In reality, nobody ever ridiculed me because I spoke one language better than the other. On the contrary, my friends loved it.

My mother's recollection of my experiences is also very positive. "Even though you couldn't speak English, you still had no problem communicating with your friends." Apparently I was a very expressive child (I suppose I still am). We've all heard that kids can be cruel, but that was not my experience at all. As scared as I was of not fitting in, I can't recall a single bad experience with my friends and classmates.

Perhaps because of this, my mother says that eventually it

was very easy for me to learn English and I continued on through my normal schooling along with everyone else. There were no special ESL (English as a second language) programs in the schools that I attended, and I was not assigned a translator or language tutor—it was sink or swim. I was forced to learn English out of necessity. I have no memory of it being a negative or tumultuous experience because nobody told me it was supposed to be. It was just something I had to do so I did it. I'm sure I struggled from an academic standpoint while I was learning the language, but I'm grateful that my parents chose not to warn me of social struggles that never came.

My childhood experiences taught me that we don't give children enough credit when it comes to adapting to new circumstances. We unnecessarily prepare them for drama and plant all kinds of warnings in their heads as a way to protect them. Yet when older kids come to America as immigrants, they know, and their parents know, that English will have to be learned. Parents make sure that their children learn English because they know they must to excel in the United States. If a healthy child running around the yard is stopped and given crutches there's a good chance that he will suddenly realize he needs them. Kids aren't going to be aware of an impending crisis unless you tell them to prepare for one. I think our mistake is that we warn and prepare our children instead of telling them that an experience is going to be an adventure. When kids are given this perspective, they're going to learn the language faster, not just because they have to, but because they want to.

At home, it was easier and only natural for my mother to speak to us in Spanish. The great thing about this was that necessity allowed me to maintain two languages at the same time. Keeping the Spanish language in my life today has a lot to do with my parents. Although they are both American citizens of more than thirty years, they are still more comfortable with their own language than with their "second language." As a family we speak to each other in Spanish. This is why I specifically teach Sofia Spanish in addition to English. I know that speaking two languages will be a great asset for her.

You might notice that I didn't refer to English as Sofia's "second language." I recently realized how Christopher and I are effectively raising her to speak and use both languages equally. I hope that this will solve the problem of balancing between both worlds that I experienced. I hope Sofia will see English and Spanish simply as two different aspects of her world, one world with many colors and options. Right now, even as a small child, she has an equal grasp of both languages. Now, imagine if all immigrant parents took this approach— teaching both languages equally without referring to one or the other as a "second language." We could literally obliterate the acronym ESL.

I have realized that the Spanish language is one of my greatest and most valuable business tools. Having two languages has allowed me to communicate with professionals and people from all walks of life and around the world. The mere fact that I am Latina and speak Spanish has led people to specifically seek me out in my professional life. I use Spanish every single day. I'm proud to say that I have an excellent command of both English and Spanish. It's a great balance. It's very clear to anyone who meets me that I am a product of both worlds.

"Los últimos serán los primeros"
(The last will be the first)
—MATTHEW 19:30

Immigrants new to America typically face a variety of language-based barriers. Being ESL affects a person's ability to make friends outside their own community. Furthermore, at work and in professional situations, not speaking perfect English often prevents immigrants from getting jobs commensurate with their experience and education. As an immigration lawyer I've noticed that when an educated man from a Spanish-speaking country opens his mouth, his education suddenly gets lost within his accent.

Difficulties speaking and understanding English sometimes keep new citizens from taking part in the political process. When politicians and candidates can speak more than one language, they can explain issues to more of their constituents. Yet voter apathy is rampant. Immigrants and nonimmigrants alike ask: What difference is my one vote going to make? If all immigrants, especially Latinos, realized the power that they have, things would change dramatically for the better.

The good news is that since my parents immigrated, these

language barriers have shifted. Professionally and economically, all types of businesses have realized the value of attracting immigrant communities. So much advertising is done in Spanish to attract international clients (and the large population of Spanish-speaking Americans). American companies are hiring immigrants because their abilities fit well into today's global marketplace. There is such a big market for bilingual professionals that it would be economically foolish to ignore the benefits of such an employee. This is especially ironic to me, because if my father were a new immigrant today looking for work in American medicine, it would be considered an advantage that he speaks Spanish.

"La ignorancia es muy atrevida"
(Ignorance is very bold)

We have developed a very hypocritical way of looking at immigrants—especially considering that we are a nation of immigrants. We generally never call famous athletes or entertainers "immigrants." Antonio Banderas is casually referred to as being "from Spain."

While kids consider the ability to speak another language as "cool" and unique, adults, conformist and set in their ways, are too often wary of diversity. When they first immigrated, my parents faced a lot of discrimination because English was their second language. In fact, I still see them facing it today, over forty years later. My father still has a beautiful accent and such an elegant way of pronouncing and saying things—not unlike actor Antonio Banderas and other bilingual celebrities. Why is it that people respect and fawn over famous Latinos while discriminating against their less well-known counterparts?

I think discrimination against immigrants is rooted in a sense of pride—"you're in my country; speak my language." An even stronger motivation is fear of the unknown. A strange language triggers a subconscious (or, unfortunately, sometimes conscious) fear of change—"This is the greatest country in the world and we must preserve it." The sentiment is right, but the behavior is not. Is this because America is such a young nation with a constantly fluctuating, unstable foundation that we believe any kind of change is a threat? Do we believe that new cultures, traditions, and languages will topple the house of cards? Or is there a guilt issue? All Americans know on some level that we are all immigrants on "borrowed land," Europeans, Asians, Africans, and Latinos alike. Maybe when a "new accent" arrives, it reminds us of all the cultural turmoil that has occurred in America's history. We wonder if yet one more accent, one more culture, will create renewed unrest on "our land." The question is, does this fear, this visceral reaction, and this long history, justify discrimination? The answer is no.

What needs to happen for America to move beyond these barriers? How can we remember what a melting pot should truly sound like?

Immigrant communities need to push more to set their

place in American history without being afraid. It's really up to us to inspire change. We must speak proudly with our accents.

Enrique's Story

"La diligencia es madre de la buena ventura"
(Diligence is the mother of good fortune)

When my friend Enrique arrived in the United States he encountered many challenges from not being able to understand English well. This was a terrible feeling for him. He recalls that it was like "living in a world of confusion." He knew that it was going to take him a while to perfect the little English he already knew, but he never felt less a man than anyone else, because his mother would not let him. He knew it would just be a matter of time, and in this way, he felt a little bit better about the situation.

Enrique spoke Spanish while most of his classmates did not. Ironically, he was more advanced academically in math, history, literature, and many other subjects. But he still felt out of place. His mother told him, as only a mother can, "All you need now is to learn the language!"

In the midst of his struggles to learn the language and communicate with his classmates, Enrique managed to find humor in some of the situations he found himself in. For instance, he initially had trouble ordering food and was too embarrassed to ask his "interpreter" to translate for him. So he would simply stand behind someone in line and wait for them to order. When it was his turn, he would ask to be given "the same," hoping that the person in front of him had ordered something good. I imagine that this was also a good way to become acquainted with some of the food in his new country!

Enrique's most trying and memorable experience occurred a few weeks after he arrived in the United States. During metal shop, he had to go to the restroom but did not know how to ask the teacher and was afraid to bother his interpreter, who also happened to be the school's bully—the "Lechero" as he was called. The Lechero was in a gang and had made his mark through graffiti all over East Los Angeles—everyone knew this guy. Faced with these two very undesirable options, Enrique decided to just walk out of the classroom to the restroom. As luck would have it, he ran into a teacher in the hallway who demanded to see his hall pass— a demand Enrique could not understand or respond to. He recalls being so afraid and repeating over and over to the teacher, "Sorry no English." Finally the teacher asked him where his classroom was and Enrique guided him there by pointing. The teacher proceeded to embarrass Enrique in front of the whole classroom by telling the metal shop instructor, "This is your student and I found him in the hall without a hall pass!" The whole class looked at him and said, "Ohhh no pass, give him a swat!" Apparently, in those days, teachers gave kids swats in the classroom when they misbehaved. Enrique tells me how they used a big *palo* (paddle) to "hit you in the butt."

The metal shop instructor yelled at Enrique in front of the whole class. Once again, he said, "No English," so the instructor asked who in the class spoke Spanish. To his chagrin, Enrique's translator, the Lechero, immediately volunteered to translate and explained to him what was happening. Enrique asked the Lechero to apologize to the teacher and say he didn't know he needed a hall pass. The Lechero translated Enrique's response to the teacher as "Hey—none of your business!" Can you believe it?

Of course the teacher was furious, but fortunately Enrique had made a sincere friendship with a boy from Guatemala. His friend instantly defended him and cleared up the translation. This worked out well, since that instructor didn't like El Lechero anyway. So the teacher ended up giving one swat to Enrique and the other to the Lechero.

After class, the Lechero's response to his swat was to tell Enrique *"¡Te voy a brincar!"* (I am going to jump you). Once again, Enrique was confused. The Lechero's threat turned out to be in something called "Spanglish." The word *brincar* to Enrique meant simply "to jump" as in "jump over" versus "jump on and beat up"—as the Lechero clearly intended to do. Sure enough, after school the Lechero was waiting to beat him up and began to run after him. Enrique remembers that he never ran away so fast in his entire life!

Enrique got home and promptly exclaimed to his mother, "We're going home to Morelia! I do not want to live in this country anymore. Someone wants to kill me!" And that is how my friend Enrique learned that the language issue would be his biggest challenge as an immigrant.

QUICK TIP

Learn English:
Latinos who are fully bilingual are more likely to enjoy success in their career.

CHAPTER SEVENTEEN

Remembering Our Roots

"El que es ciego de nación, nunca sabe por dónde anda"
(He who is blind to his own nation
will never know where he is traveling)

Immigrants come to the United States to discover opportunities better than those available in their own countries. However, sometimes they're so consumed with this objective that they start to lose their own language and culture to become "American." The greatest challenge in this situation is being aware of our natural tendency. The cycle starts with an immigrant trying to escape the American immigrant stereotype and ends with the individual stripping their true identity just to "fit in" for fear of discrimination. For many, that fear becomes a motivating factor in risking individuality and culture to become something they're not.

I too faced this challenge, and looking back I now wish that I had been prouder as a child of my identity. I've always been proud of who I am, but I wish I had listened a lot sooner to what my mother and father were telling me. I wish I hadn't tried to hash out a different identity when I didn't need to. I already had my true identity, derived from what they instilled in me. All I needed to do was perfect it. Today I consider it a triumph that I have followed this lesson from my parents. I wish I could help other people realize how valuable it is to be part of another culture. There is so much more we can do because we are bicultural.

I am an American Latina. I was born in America as a Latina. I am also a mother, a wife, a daughter, a sister, and a professional. I've also been able to use Spanish and all the values I've learned from my Colombian culture to benefit America. I have put what some people consider to be negatives to work as positives in my professional life to help others. I'm so proud that I can use these gifts on a daily basis, turning negative stereotypes into positive values that people can live by.

It should come as no surprise to learn that my parents were responsible for teaching me to successfully integrate our native culture with our new life in America. With their deep sense of tradition, my parents taught me that you can use the "old school" with the new in every situation. More importantly, I learned that our conduct at home should be exactly the same in public.

To experience the same traditions that my mother and father did when they were growing up and then share them with my own family is proof that children truly are *"la prolongación de nuestra existencia"* (the prolongation of our existence). It's amazing to me that my daughter, at such a young age, is able to understand the difference between her two languages. She knows who to speak to in Spanish and who in English. This really shows how kids are human sponges—she just understands. She may not understand culture yet, but she clearly understands that we are who we are. Sofia sees how great it is to be surrounded by a lot of people all the time. She has always lived in a busy environment with new people, and likes that aspect of our family and her culture. Through her family's example, Sofia has learned that there is so much to her history.

"El mundo es de lo valientes"
(The world belongs to the brave)

To work in the United States demands a lot from anyone, male or female. Long hours, especially when you're trying to establish and prove yourself, take time away from your family. As a woman, many of us have the added pressure of household responsibilities to deal with.

On the bright side, one of my favorite things about America is the beauty of its landscapes, especially here in California where the desert, beach, and ski slopes are accessible within mere hours of each other. In spite of the stereotypes about immigrant overcrowding, we still manage to make room for everybody who wants to be here. All the misinformation has not affected this country's ability to thrive. It is continuously revitalized by each new wave of immigrants and the cultures they bring. Those who don't know any better often attempt to stop this natural growth and lead immigrants to believe that they are unwanted and that there are very limited opportunities here, when in fact the opposite is true. What if immigrants really started to use the power they have? America is a ready, willing, level playing field just waiting for that to happen. I guess you could say that opportunity runs in our national family. As my father always says, "anything is possible in America . . . the opportunities are limitless."

All immigrants, new and old, should be excited about these opportunities! Know that you as an individual can create your own little niche here. Bring your culture and make it work for you. Your uniqueness will lead you to success. Find your own identity, be happy with it, and incorporate it into every facet of your life.

I will admit that the "cultural identity" balancing act gets harder every day, but we are in America and we should be proud to be here. Embrace everything that this country has to offer. We should continue to respect our own traditions but also incorporate bits of America into them. I personally don't think that welcoming new traditions dishonors our own cultures. Instead, I think it only reinforces them.

I had the opportunity to counsel a Latino boy, another Enrique, who confided that he was embarrassed by his family's culture, to the point that he wanted to change his name to be like his American friends. I tried to explain that even if he changed his name he would still have dark skin, dark hair, and the essence of his identity would never change. I told him to be proud of his traditions and culture. I asked him if he knew that Latinos go to war, fight, and die for this country as heroes. I asked him if he knew that as a Latino he may have more of an opportunity to succeed than someone who doesn't speak another language. I also asked him if he really wanted to be just like everybody else. America is about being a unique individual. Why would he throw away something so great? There is a dicho that says *"No dar uno el brazo a torcer"* (Don't let anything twist your arm). As my dad described this particular situation, "This young man let someone compromise his identity." Someone had given him an inferiority complex by making him be embarrassed by his parents' accents. Now this feeling was causing him to think about giving up the best part of himself.

Another great example of this lesson is when my friend Enrique's college counselor gave him some valuable advice for defending his identity and his name. She told him, "Remember no matter what happens in life you are Enrique Arevalo. Never change the pronunciation of your name for anyone. Spell it out for them if they do not understand it. Do not make it easy for anyone." She taught him to have faith in himself no matter what.

All the many Latinos who only speak Spanish, especially the famous athletes and movie stars, are not embarrassed by their culture. They know that if you change your identity, you change who you are. Staying true to both aspects of yourself—old and new—is the truly courageous decision. What I learned from my parents and what I have taught

Sofia is *"El mundo es de los valientes"* (The world belongs to the brave).

My courageous friend Enrique is a great inspiration in this regard. He has used his culture, family lessons, and roots as tools for success rather than hindrances or obstacles. He is the perfect example of an immigrant using his identity to his advantage.

Like many before him, Enrique faced discrimination that he needed to overcome. He felt it back then and often tells me how he still feels it today. I agree when he tells me that immigrants cannot let these challenges distract them from their goals. Just as my father continued to become a doctor, despite having to deal with discrimination.

Enrique says that he has never let discrimination bother him or make him feel like a victim. He has never felt like an alien or a stranger in this country. He has always made a point of learning its history and has always felt that this country offered equal opportunity to everybody.

"La justicia cojea, pero llega"
(Justice limps but it gets there)

When it comes to serving others, I believe you must reach beyond yourself and your daily commitments. Find a passion to make not only your life but also your community better. I truly believe that every person, regardless of economic stature, should dedicate time to assist someone or benefit some cause. Get involved. Get out there. Get motivated!

A common question I am asked is, "Where does your energy come from?" The answer is simple—from the example my parents set, from the passion I have for my career, from my opportunity to reach out to people every day through television, and from the love of my community and its culture.

With my immigrant parents' examples to follow, it is easy to understand my passion for practicing immigration law. After all, America is a nation of all kinds of immigrants. Throughout its history, this country has been a beacon of freedom and tolerance, a land of opportunity for all to succeed. The strength of this country is found in the variety of cultures and traditions that immigrants bring to it. If we forget this, we lose that strength.

My practice allows me to help immigrants integrate into the American heritage. From business professionals, athletes, artists, musicians, and entertainers, to the cook who makes your breakfast or lunch each and every day at your favorite restaurant. Immigrating to this country is complicated and time consuming. It requires the expenditure of a considerable amount of energy and emotion. This leaves many immigrants feeling disconnected and discouraged, but somehow they find the endurance to keep going. Despite the struggles and negative stereotypes of immigrants, most never give up because of the deep love they have for their adopted country. Let me tell you, there are no words to truly describe the feeling of being part of someone's dream, being part of helping people establish their lives as hard-working citizens in this country. With each client, there is someone who always reminds me of my family's story—my immigrant roots.

CHAPTER EIGHTEEN

America: The Great Patchwork Quilt

"Pueblo dividido, pueblo vencido"
(A people divided is a people conquered)

America—a grand patchwork quilt that people sometimes confuse with a single-colored throw blanket. It keeps us vibrant, while maintaining the energy, flexibility, and resilience of our national personality. Our immigrants are the reason we have an intimate connection with the rest of the world.

The United States has derived its great power from its diversity. Immigrants laid the framework for this nation with their blood, sweat, and tears. Without exception, immigrants of the past are viewed with respect and gratitude. So why are modern-day immigrants held in such contempt? We should certainly be able to live on the same street together as Italian, German, Mexican and all other families, just as early immigrants managed (for the most part) to cohabitate in the cramped neighborhoods of New York City and other overcrowded cities.

Immigrant contributions to the security of our nation and to our democracy are well documented. For example, one third of all presidential Medals of Honor have been awarded to Latinos. Immigrants are patriotic Americans who are willing to fight for freedom. Many serve in the military before they are citizens. Today there are over twenty thousand legal permanent residents enlisted in our nation's armed forces protecting our airports, seaports, and borders. Immigrants risk their lives daily around the world to protect us here at home.

Beyond the dollars and cents, immigrants bring many benefits to America. Their numerous accomplishments range from those of foreign-born United States Olympic champions, to Madeline Albright's (Czechoslovakia), who was the sixty-fourth secretary of state and one of the highest-ranking women ever in the history of the U.S. government. Albert Einstein (Germany) and Alexander Graham Bell (Scotland) were some of the most exceptional individuals in their fields and accolades given to them have brought honor and prestige to this country. Did you know that between 1901 and 1991, forty-four of the one hundred Nobel Prizes awarded to American researchers were won by immigrants or their children?

However, many anti-immigrant groups would like the

American public to believe that today's immigrants make up a static community that exists in a vicious cycle of poverty from which they are unlikely to escape. Yet history has proven that immigrants generally come to the United States to give their children better opportunities. Their expectations for them to succeed often propel children of immigrants to reach for something beyond their current situation.

In the wake of September 11, 2001, while America has responded with a greater commitment to freedom, there are those who use these tragic events to propose that in the name of national security, America should close itself off from the rest of the world. Proposals range from quadrupling the number of border agents to building the "great wall of America" across our entire southern border. But we fail to recognize that the problem is not immigration but terrorism. How can immigrants who contribute so much to our society hurt us?

Our immigration laws, designed to be fair to immigrants from all over the world, have gotten tougher over the years. Why? Because of fear-based, inaccurate, negative stereotypes associated with these newcomers—they're lazy criminals who take jobs from hard-working Americans, and who deplete our resources. In reality, immigrants are extremely hard-working people. But of course every cultural group has good, bad, lazy, and hard-working members. But why is it that only immigrants are singled out by such uninformed prejudice, in the one country where all should be welcomed and accepted? Are we that afraid of competition? Perhaps we're using this fear to justify discrimination, but this misrepresents what America is all about.

Ironically, when my parents immigrated, the laws allowed for more immigration but more discrimination also existed. There was, and still is a fear that immigrants will spoil this country. Another irony is that famous people have an easier time with immigration laws. We make it attractive for athletes and actors to immigrate, but a challenge for nurses, teachers, and scientists—professionals that we need desperately. Immigration laws don't seem to reward the everyday hard-working people who make our country great. What does that say about America's work values and priorities? This attitude has crossed over into the inherent discrimination of our immigration laws. Why are we falling so far behind in education that our nation is beginning to lag in science and technology? Why are our kids unwilling to work as hard as past generations? Is it because we are preventing the hardest-working individuals, those who could improve our work ethic, from even entering the country? We should be embracing and celebrating these values, instead of discriminating against them. Imagine what a positive message we'd be sending to our children!

Our laws vary, of course, according to the immigrant's nationality, profession, family relationship, and situation. To be fair, as a nation we are sympathetic to those with unique circumstances. For example, we offer protective statuses for people from countries in civil war and natural disaster victims. But it's important to remember that whatever their specific circumstance, all immigrants arrive in America with a clean slate, ready to attain a level of success that they probably could not have reached in their home country.

I feel that my friend Enrique, like my father, is the embodiment of the courage needed to leave your country, come here, and risk everything to attain the American Dream. It takes tremendous patience, tolerance, and open mindedness to immigrate and succeed in a new country. Their stories are typical of so many others in our country. Every immigrant story is the same in some ways.

Enrique tells me that he did not plan to be an immigrant. In fact, he was very happy in Mexico until the age of fourteen. He remembers how all his relatives from the United States often visited his family which was living happily in Mexico. His father had many aunts and uncles who lived in the United States, mostly in California and Arizona, so Enrique knew there must be a connection between living in Mexico and living in America. Suddenly the United States was no longer a far-off, foreign country. Meanwhile, business in Mexico was not good. Enrique's father owned a cargo truck business that hauled goods from one city to another. He was experiencing problems, getting too old, and competition was very stiff. So eventually, his father temporarily came to the United States to make more money while his family patiently waited for him in Mexico. His father arrived in 1963 (the same year my own parents, Darío and Aracelly, arrived in the Bronx) when he was in his early thirties and Enrique was around ten years old. His father ended up working in Albuquerque, New Mexico, because that was where his padrino (godfather) lived. Enrique's father would send his family money, all the while calling and writing to tell them all how much he hated being in the United States without his family and how he wanted to return to Mexico to see them. There are countless versions of Enrique's story in cities all across the United States.

As these immigrants successfully assimilate, they still bring a little of their own country, helping us create who we are as a nation. Think about it—little Tokyo, little Italy, Chinatown, etc. America is a place where anyone can come and feel right at home.

> *Give me your tired, your poor,*
> *Your huddled masses yearning to breathe free,*
> *The wretched refuse of your teeming shore.*
> *Send these, the homeless, tempest-tossed to me.*
> *I lift my lamp beside the golden door.*
>
> —EMMA LAZARUS
>
> (INSCRIBED ON THE STATUE OF LIBERTY)

America is the only country in the world that has communicated overwhelmingly powerful messages of openness and acceptance throughout our history. You may have heard that "there's no more room at the inn" in our country. Can you imagine what would happen if that were really true? What a sad end that would be to such a great story.

I can't wait to take Sofia to visit the Statue of Liberty. I can't wait for her to feel the immense power and pride in being at the top of this symbol. I can't wait for her to feel acceptance, and a magical, indescribable sense of nationalism. I hope that her Statue of Liberty experience reinforces the fact that she lives in the greatest country in the world, and that this magnificent lady was given to us because we stand for liberty.

SECTION VII

Living by Los Dichos

CHAPTER NINETEEN

Living for the Moment

*"No podemos posponer la vida hasta que estemos listos. La
característica más importante de la vida es su urgencia"*
(We are not able to postpone living until we are ready; the
most important characteristic of life is urgency)

—José Ortega y Gasset

This is not a dicho but a valuable lesson I once heard. Living for the moment means that the ride up the ladder is the best part. Enjoy every day and try your best not to become obsessed with the finish line. A wonderful story called "The Station" by Robert Hastings demonstrates this point well. The story describes how we are so obsessed with the final destination—whether it is turning eighteen or twenty-one, finishing school, getting the house or car of our dreams, or retiring—that we fail to realize that the "true joy in life is the trip." The moments from point A to point B are the real ones, and therefore the most valuable. The station, as Hastings says, "is only a dream." Water comes and water goes away, but the moments we create for ourselves and live within, remain.

How do you create these moments in your own life? Make things happen! Reach beyond yourself. Look outside of your comfort zone. Don't sit around expecting things to happen for you or to you, and don't be depressed if you have not met your goals. Continue to put effort into your family, relationships, and most important, yourself. Set your eyes on a goal, respect it with compassion, prepare for it, and then achieve it. True success takes time. You are the only person responsible for your success and failures. Don't blame anyone else. As one of my favorite dichos says, *"Honra y dinero se ganan despacio y se pierden ligero"* (Reputation and money are earned slowly but lost quickly).

Each day we stroll off to work or our destination for the day with the assumption that today is a certainty and tomorrow will surely follow. In some respects that simple mind-set adheres to the notion of complacency rather than vigor and zest for the moment. Then in an instant the world of our mind's eye can be immediately altered. Most of us have experienced an altering, so-called life-changing experience, and all of us have matured because of it. Whether that experience is considered tragic or a blessing, it becomes a memorable snapshot in one's life forever. These instances make us change. If we fail to do so we may enter a mind-set of mediocrity.

Such a memorabe experience occurred in my family. You may recall the story of "The Dukes" and my father-in-law, Ray. In 2001, Ray died shortly after being diagnosed with pancreatic cancer. This story about Ray shows how every moment of life means something and that a close-knit family and group of friends have to support each other in a time of crisis. Above all, it is a story that proves the fragility of life. We must realize how important it is to enjoy every moment you are blessed to spend with your family and loved ones.

My brother José went to medical school outside of the United States, just as my father did. José had a close-knit group of friends in medical school, including a friend named Eric. During their time in medical school, José and Eric spent some time in New York City for their residency. Once my father-in-law, Ray, a traveling toy salesman, was in New York, and with my help, looked up José and hosted a very Dukes-like night on the town for José and Eric. Ray picked up the two in a town car, and boy, did they ever paint the town red! This night had such an impact that José still talks about it today. Having known Ray and heard all the old Dukes stories from my husband, I can only imagine how much fun they had that night.

Flash forward to 2001 when my dear father-in-law, after having been ill for quite some time, was in the Veterans Hospital in Loma Linda, California, sicker than ever. Who walks in the room as his doctor to treat him? Eric! Ray was very sick and did not immediately recognize him, but Eric quickly recounted their evening out in New York City, telling Ray how much fun he and José had and that they still appreciated it to that day. Ray then remembered and the two reminisced. The reunion was cut short, however, after Eric examined Ray, put him through some tests, and knew the prognosis was dire. Eric did not tell Ray. Rather, he immediately called my father, and told him what he believed the tests revealed.

My father called my husband and told him to go to Loma Linda, pick up his father, and bring him to his office—right then. Hearing what he heard in my father's voice, Christopher did so, no questions asked. After reviewing the X-rays and examining Ray, my father came to our house that night and told Christopher: "If I ever expect you do something, this is it. Be with your father. Your father needs you now more than ever . . . he has cancer and he's going to die." This must have been so daunting for my father the surgeon and cancer specialist to tell Christopher, his son-in-law, such horrible, heartbreaking news. Without knowing too much, Christopher said to my father, "Okay, Darío, I understand."

It was soon decided by the cancer specialist that it was my father who should tell Ray the news. By then Ray was very ill and even before the diagnosis, the Dukes arrived to rally around him. They seemed to know that something bad was happening. Until the day Ray died, the Dukes flooded our home and his with love, compassion, laughter, and stories. The outpouring of love was intense and uplifting.

I will always remember exactly who was in the room— Ray, my husband and I, my father, and of course the Dukes. I still remember where each person was sitting and every other detail of that night in the living room when my father delivered the news. Ray, insisting that the diagnosis, whatever it was, come from a family member, said to Darío, "Give it to me straight," and looked him in the eye—the unflinching epitome of a macho man. My father looked at Ray and said,

"You have pancreatic cancer and you're dying." All Ray did was nod. Everyone else in the room, however—myself included—was a mess. My father told Ray that he had anywhere from three weeks to ninety days left to live. This statement woke my husband up from the "daily grind" he had been subjecting himself to. My father later told Christopher, "If there's anything you ever wanted to know about your father, now is the time to ask."

It is said that pancreatic cancer is the most painful and the quickest to take somebody's life. In a sense it is almost a sign of God's divine plan that the most painful type of cancer progresses the fastest so the person does not suffer for long. From our point of view as his family, however, it was just terrible that Ray would soon be leaving us.

That was both the best and worst of times. The best was that we were able to spend that time with Ray. After his diagnosis, he and my mother-in-law, Josephine, stayed with us for a few weeks. The house was full. The time spent with him felt both incredible and surreal—a feeling you know you can't touch. The worst occurred as we all watched this strong, iron man slowly lose his personality because this disease was taking him away. You have to understand a little about Ray and his vigor for life. Ray was a man—"The Man," to be exact. He was smart, handsome, vivacious, and engaging, and had the greatest personality. Unknowingly, when he walked into a room he immediately commanded it. Everyone was drawn to him. That's what made this even more infuriating. How dare this disease suck the energy out of this absolutely amazing person?

When he died my husband and I helped my mother-in-law sort through Ray's belongings. We discovered boxes and boxes of pictures and scrapbooks—mostly of the Dukes. We looked at these little devilish decked-out men and could only imagine the stories behind the photos. I have never seen so many photos in my entire life. What's interesting is that I never really took pictures before that and now we take them constantly. I try to take advantage of every single moment and capture it on film, especially moments with my daughter, Sofia. Those photos were Ray's lesson to us from Heaven—this is how you need to live life. Even today I believe that he is my guardian angel. His death taught us all how to live in the moment with so much more passion and vigor.

Ray was a man who knew how to seize the day. He was a light that everyone was drawn to. He lived life for the moment. He lived for his children, wife, and friends. He welcomed everyone. Christopher's friends became his friends. When he passed away, I was amazed to see how many of Christopher's friends expressed how close they felt to him. Some even wished Ray was their father—in essence, he was.

I know that I'm also speaking for Ray and everyone who knew him when I say that I hope each of you reading this right now learns to live for the moment every day. This may sound a little morbid and the advice may sound easy, but it is not. We all have other things going on. Many times we are thinking about what will be next, or thinking about some past event. If you spend any time regretting the past or worrying about the future, you leave no room for the present. Focus on the present. When you see a challenge, attack it right then. Do not wait. For if you do, you may miss an opportunity to grow.

Next time you speak with someone, pay close attention to where your mind is. Are you thinking about what they are saying or are you anticipating your response? If so, you are missing the moment. When you bring your awareness into the moment, all worries of the past and all perceived fears of the future fade away. In this frame of mind you are able to see life clearly.

In fact, as I write this we continue to journey through the trials and tribulations of Ray's death and how it affected our family. However, we have been able to find solace in the simple things in life again, and I ask each of you to do the same at all times and in everything you do. The next time you do anything, whether in solitude or with family and friends, stop, and enjoy the moment—the scenery, sounds, smells, and most important, enjoy the people you are with. Do not take this time for granted. Seize every moment for it is only in that instant that great things occur.

Ray taught us that everything can wait except health, happiness, and family. I wish that he could be here to see Sofia. I am the most present when I'm with my daughter—reading a book, talking to her, playing. It's so easy to be present when you are relishing the world of a child. Children are truly the only beings on this planet who are present all of the time. Look at them as they talk to their friends (even the imaginary ones), and play. They are always so engrossed in exactly what they are doing exactly when they are doing it that it's sometimes nearly impossible to get their attention. Instead of being frustrated by this (especially on the tenth call to dinner) we should be inspired by it. Children know that we are present when our minds are focused on something enjoyable. Their laughter is contagious and therapeutic. Like my mother says, *"La riza es un remedio infalible"* (Laughter is the best medicine).

Just as I have talked throughout this book about all the lessons we should be passing on to our children, this is a lesson that they are uniquely qualified to teach to us. There is so much we can learn from them and this is one of the most important things. This has brought the whole book around full circle—advice from a mother to a daughter all the way to advice from a daughter to a mother.

I close this chapter with a message to Ray: I will always teach my children and others to live life as you did—with zest for life, with unending love and eternal happiness, and most important, to live in the present as you did, for the moment and without a single regret. Ray, I miss you, love you, and dedicate this saying to you: *"El cielo es donde estarás cuando te sientas bien donde estás ahora"* (Heaven is where you will be when you are happy with where you are now).

QUICK TIP

Be positive:

Focus on the power of the present. Take hold of the moment. Be grateful for people and events that you have in your life today—not yesterday, not tomorrow.

CHAPTER TWENTY

Living by Los Dichos

"Del dicho al hecho hay mucho trecho"
(It is a long way from the saying to the doing)

Dichos and proverbs communicate family values and traditions; they mold and define us. I hope you have seen for yourself how the selected dichos represent, embody, and elaborate on the material covered in every section. I chose the dichos and pieces of family wisdom that mean the most to me and have had the most value in my life. Dichos teach and direct you toward the most important things—family, relationships, identity, and being true to yourself.

The most beautiful thing for me is how all of these dichos are tightly tied to tradition. They each have profound meanings that made sense twenty generations ago and still do today.

Great values are strong, undeniable, and will always be around. You can't argue with tradition—it's an impossible argument to win.

Then why reinvent the wheel that our ancestors created? Of course we have to carve out our own identities but there's nothing wrong with admitting that a large part of our identity comes from our parents and grandparents. The saying "you have to find your own way in life" doesn't mean that you're cheating when you use tradition and family values to help you along.

Personally, I have learned so much from writing this book and revisiting all the wonderful wisdom I have received from my family over the years. One of my favorite dichos, and the one that best describes my lessons learned during this process, is the one I used to open this chapter. While writing some of the earliest chapters of this book, I suddenly became aware of how I had largely forgotten these lessons over the years. I've been working so hard trying to be perfect in all of my roles—professional, mother, wife, daughter—that I am guilty of blending all the roles into one without taking the time to enjoy each individually. I need to take my own advice! I don't have to be infallible in everything, everywhere, and every moment. I have learned that I am a human being and am allowed to make mistakes. I don't always have to find all the solutions all the time. There are so many things that I've learned and know, but have yet to use in my life. Writing this book has been a true awakening in all aspects of my life. I make it a point every day to remember everything my parents have taught me and think of ways to use my knowledge. I hope that writing this book will make me better in all my roles, including my role as a human being—flaws and all.

I am now acutely aware of the power and knowledge I have and I know how to use it to view life in a more positive, full, and appreciative way. If I could just take my own advice, relax and listen to the things that I'm telling others, I would be a much better person. I am so grateful for the life I have—a life based on tradition, created by good hard work, that others could take for granted. I appreciate that I come from a very ambitious family with a strong moral base that I know will never fail me. So I take the good with the bad, because the good overshadows the bad. I've learned not to look at anything as a negative in life.

The original intention of this book was to select the dichos passed down to me from my family, particularly my mother, that have most affected and guided my life, interpret the dichos, and translate them into solid advice. At the end of this journey, looking back, it appears that I may have gone beyond that original intention. What ended up happening was that as I pored through list after list of dichos from my memory and those contributed by my mother, I became aware of the deeper connections and meanings of these dichos. I observed their connection to history, present-day society, my own family stories, our cultural past, and saw how all of this can tie into any reader's life—from home to the office and into the future.

I have learned that the older you get, the younger you become. As the years go by, (this book was a little bit like aging) the more you realize how you need only the basic things in life. The older I get, the more I realize that the most valuable things in life are also the simplest and don't cost a thing. This has indeed been a journey of simplicity and clarity. Somewhere within the complications of writing a book, sorting through all these dichos, proverbs, and cultural wisdom, life's most valuable and important messages have been simplified for me. In the midst of it all, I have learned that your heart and your gut are always right.

Learning, and living, by *los dichos* is a continual process, a constant daily cycle. There is never a finality to this wisdom. There is always something to be done and learned in life. Just like our children, we need to learn something new every day to improve ourselves and understand life a little bit better. I encourage you to share your journey of wisdom with your children. Pass down dichos or your own cultural wisdom so that they may do the same, and this cultural core will never die.

What has been your personal experience in reading this book? Did it remind you of your life journey and the wisdom that your own family has passed on to you (or at least attempted to)? I hope you have discovered what is most important about your life and what defines you—your unique identity. Maybe you knew about your unique identity before but never knew what a gift it is—your language, parents, family greatness. What is the one thing in your life that is good and worth struggling for? I hope that it is something good and valuable about yourself. I hope it's in your heart, and I hope it's connected to your family traditions in some way.

No matter what race or sex you are or what part of the

world you live in, it is easy to understand what the most important thing is in every culture—family. The core of every community and the core of our essence as human beings since the beginning of time, from birth, until death, revolves around family. When we devalue the importance of family and try to make it casual, we deny a universal truth that has met the test of time. I have especially learned from writing the family chapters of this book that the idea of family being "casual" is harmful to any society that has this point of view. My wish for you, the reader, is to realize this and strengthen society simply by cementing your own family bonds. If we, as individual families, are not casual, then society won't be either. Strengthening society starts in *our* homes. If we can recognize that all cultures have the same familial center, then we can finally look at each other as more than strangers. Kinship is all about that basic individual bond with our own families. The world really is a level playing field when it consists of family values and traditions.

If you feel lost, I hope that this book has given you something to connect to and believe in—a core that leads you back to yourself. Hopefully this will inspire you to return to and connect with your family, culture, and ancestry in a way that you never thought possible. I hope you see that whether you knew it or not, they were there the whole time waiting for you.

Afterword

A letter to our daughter Cristina
from
Aracelly and Darío Pérez

To our beloved Cristina,

One day we will depart to a better life, so it is important for us to know that we made an impact on your life, your brother's and sister's lives, our grandchildren's lives, and the lives of all those others whom we've come in contact with. We are very proud to have accomplished our mission and are sure that God blessed us with the necessary guidance and direction to become true representatives of His life and world.

We realized our dream, our American Dream. Looking back it was difficult but never impossible. Today, we understand what we accomplished and are amazed. Wow! How could we have done this? We can only attribute our success to our own parents, you, and your brother and sister, who have always been the central focus of our lives.

In South America in the 1940s it was common for our

mothers to stay home and raise the family. They were directly responsible for our education. Miguel de Unamuno once said, *"No se como puede vivir quien no lleve a flor de alma los recuerdos de su niñez"* (I do not know how one can live without taking to heart memories of your childhood). Our childhood was filled with such beautiful memories created by our parents. A typical tool that they used to teach and educate was dichos. While they may have not realized it, those dichos imparted invaluable family wisdom and traditions.

A dicho is a word or group of words through which one expresses a sentiment or idea, like a proverb. Dichos are ingenious in that they always provide a valuable lesson. Dichos are the summary of human wisdom accumulated over centuries. To tell dichos is essential to express wisdom. You heard dichos from us, your relatives, and your grandparents thousands of times. They unconsciously became a part of your daily life and guided you through many good and bad times. Some of our favorites include:

> *"El que entre la miel anda, algo se le pega"*
> (You inherit the characteristics, good and bad, of the people you associate with)

> *"Dime con quién andas y te diré quién eres"*
> (Tell me the company you keep and I'll tell you the person you are)

> *"Con la vara que mides, serás medido"*
> (How you judge others is how you will be judged)

"Haz bien y no mires a quién"
(Do good and expect nothing in return)

"Árbol que crece torcido, nunca se endereza"
(A tree born crooked never straightens)

Looking back on our childhood, we believe that initially we did not understand how important dichos are. But as we grew older and wiser and were faced with confronting life on our own, flashbacks of dichos made us teach you as our own parents taught us. We are privileged to pass on to you and our grandchildren the wisdom of our ancestors and life experiences. Through this tradition as well as many others, we hope to convey how important it is to respect the strong family tie that binds us all. And more important, to reinforce the basic principles of life—love, honesty, respect, trust, protection of family, and help to those less privileged.

The love your grandparents gave us, their sacrifices for us, and the solid moral background they instilled in us helped us confront and overcome multiple and endless challenges throughout life. At times it was easier to deal with difficult moments knowing that whatever the outcome, we would succeed as a result of what they taught us. Thanks to their strong traditions, courage, and commitment we can proudly say, *"Papá y mamá, somos la prolongación de sus vidas y las extenderemos para siempre"* (Papa and Mama, we are the prolongation of your lives and we will extend them forever).

We now understand that dichos were the perfect tool to teach you how to tackle daily situations. Dichos teach one to think before acting. You must be able to analyze to understand the meaning of a dicho and this skill will always keep you ahead in the game of life. Our family wisdom, at times told through dichos, shaped our lives in a profound way. Your grandparents provided us with a solid moral foundation, devoted endless time to our well-being, growth, and development, gave us uncompromising love and sacrifice, and the best education possible. We can proudly state that these examples directly impacted the way we raised you, your sister, and your brother.

You, Cristina, have always been very inquisitive. You have always wanted to know more—about everything. From childhood, you were fascinated with dichos and their underlying messages. It was your idea to use dichos in your daily life. It seems only natural for you to write a book about what each dicho means to you and how each affects your life.

We believe that your background, upbringing, and strong family ties uniquely give you a solid foundation. We cannot ignore that your intelligence, resolve, decisiveness, and motivation to always take one more step forward also shaped your character. These qualities propelled you to achieve your dreams and become a success. But it is your compassion for others, your belief in the goodness of others, your candidness, your charm, your passion, your resounding belief in loyalty, and your sense of humor that shaped your spirit. This is what has made you an exceptional woman, daughter, sister, friend, wife, and mother. We are proud of your accomplishments and what the future holds for you and we love you.

Te amamos,
Papi y Mami

A Letter to Sofia

Dear Sofia,

I hope you realize that you truly are an inspiration to me. You have helped me understand what's most important in my life. It's not how much I have and it's not how much I do. It's how I do it that's important. I have learned that when I make mistakes I feel it more for you than for myself, because it's so important that you're proud of your mother. You've taught me to laugh and enjoy myself. You've taught me to live for the moment (to live for the graham cracker in my "coffee cup"). You've reminded me that I have to be really true to myself. It's your touch and your face that makes me feel better when I have problems. As a parent, I have an overwhelming feeling of love and admiration for you. You are the one who tells me through your words and actions that "It's okay, mama" when I'm not so sure it is. It is that feeling of utter love and joy that I never knew existed before I had you. It is such a different type of love.

Someday when you become a mother you too will understand how having and raising a child makes you complete. It brings life around full circle. You become a fulfilled human being when you become responsible for a young person. Everything you do and everything you say is a reflection of this little person who is also a reflection of yourself. I see the simplicity in your eyes and realize that you have become my teacher and I your student. You have made me value the most basic things in life. When I stumble, you make me look at myself in the mirror every day to make sure I am following the right path.

Here I am the educator trying to teach you the basics of life—good manners, values, morals, and so on. And while I'm educating you I'm reeducating and reawakening myself to the basics of my life. You, Sofia, are the only one who could do that for me. You have inspired me to look at myself and improve myself.

I hope that from this book you learn about your history and your identity. Blood carries love and tradition. I hope that you someday can learn to live by the same dichos that my mother taught me and that I'll teach you. Know that you are someone who has so much to offer because of your culture, that you should be proud of your culture, and that your culture should always be a source of confidence for you. Knowing all this means that you have already won a lot of battles and that you are way ahead of the game. *"Con el Corazón en la mano"* (With my heart in my hand) I hope that this book teaches you to be surer than ever of yourself, of your identity, and of your purpose.

Un beso,
Mamá

Bibliography

Childress, Sarah. "Made in America: Watch out, Bill Gates. Women who immigrate to the West are finding success in their new homelands by starting their own businesses." *Newsweek,* November 14, 2005.

Cisneros, Sandra. *Caramelo.* New York: Vintage, 2003.

Correa, Molina Hernando. *Refranes y Modismos Antioquenos.* Medellín: Editorial Lealon, 2004.

Londono, Agustín Jaramillo. *Testamento del paisa.* Medellín: Susaeta Ediciones, 1988.

Nava, Yolanda. *It's All in the Frijoles.* New York: Simon & Schuster, 2000.

Pearce, Susan C., Ph.D. "Today's Immigrant Woman Entrepreneur." *Immigration Policy in Focus* volume 4, issue I. American Immigration Law Foundation, January 2005.

Pérez, Aracelly. *Dichos used to raise three children with.* The House of Aracelly, 1968–present.

Con cariño

Many thanks to the American Immigration Lawyer's Association and the American Immigration Law Foundation.

To my editor, Johanna Castillo at Simon & Schuster/Atria Books, for the opportunity, support, guidance, encouragement, and for believing in me and believing that there is an audience for this book.

To Judith Curr, executive vice president and publisher of Simon & Schuster/Atria Books for her sincerity and belief in me as a first-time author.

Special thanks to my friend Christine Whitmarsh, whose creativity motivated me to push myself. Without her, I never would have thought I had it in me to write a book. She taught me that doing this was as simple as my heart told me it would be.

To my girls at the office—thanks for supporting me.

I thank my friend Enrique Arevalo for his selflessness in

sharing the most personal details about his immigration experience so I could share his story and inspire others. He knew that putting others ahead of himself would be for the greater good and as an immigrant he wanted to show the world how one person can really make a difference.

To Lori Jo, for teaching me how friendship should endure through the years.

To my law school friends Karen and Toni, thanks for always reminding me that our friendship deserves time from the daily grind.

Thank you to my girlfriend Chula, for her constant belief in me. She is a source of support and is the perfect embodiment of one of my favorite dichos: *"La amistad sincera es un alma repartida en dos cuerpos"* (True friendship is one soul shared by two bodies).

To "Ya Ya"—thank you for making our lives easier and the constant encouragement to just do it.

To my cousin Dr. Angela Arango, for reminding me that whatever comes from our hearts and personalities is really in our blood. She has also taught me that the most precious gifts we have are the gifts we have inside of ourselves. Thank you, Angie.

Thank you to my cousin Nat for always taking on the extra pressure and stress to make me better in my career. She is the true definition of a successful person—someone who is always constantly willing to help others.

To Humberto Gray, my best friend—I thank you for teaching me what friendship really means and for your guidance and inspiration. You make me believe that I can do whatever I want to do.

A heartfelt thank you to my sister, Claudia, and my brother, José, my guides in life. In a way this book is written for and about them because we are all the products of Darío and Aracelly Pérez—all for one and one for all! I am so appreciative of how they let me just be their sister. They're as proud of me as my parents are and they show that selflessly and unconditionally.

And especially to my sister, Claudia, for being a great role model of what a mother and a beautiful woman should be.

To all of my family—each and every one of them symbols of our culture because they teach me, and keep me grounded in our traditions. My family reminds me what's important and for that, I thank them all.

To Jo Jo, for sharing her contagious enthusiasm so willingly and for bringing laughter into our home.

I thank my husband, my partner in life. Yes, Christopher represents the typical macho man, but that has never once gotten in the way of his pushing and encouraging me to be better than what I am every day. He is never afraid that any success I have may overshadow him. Is that self-esteem or self-confidence? I call it true love.

Writing this book was a journey of rediscovering myself and the things that are important to me. It was also much more than that. It was a newfound appreciation for all the people around me, especially my parents. When I first talked to them about writing this book, they were so supportive. Everything you've read is a sincere and direct product of their teachings. These lessons are the core of who they are and most important what I have inherited from them.

I could write a library full of volumes of their lessons, as could anyone who was raised by incredible parents. And although it is actually a small reflection of those volumes, this book is a true celebration of everything that my parents have taught me, my sister, and my brother. Ultimately my parents, Darío and Aracelly Pérez, are the ones I really have to thank because they are at the root of everything I have learned in my life. I will always appreciate and love them for it.